Mass Media in
Black Africa

Dennis L. Wilcox

The Praeger Special Studies program—utilizing the most modern and efficient book production techniques and a selective worldwide distribution network—makes available to the academic, government, and business communities significant, timely research in U.S. and international economic, social, and political development.

Mass Media in 162096 Black Africa

Philosophy and Control

P92
A4 W5

PRAEGER SPECIAL STUDIES IN INTERNATIONAL POLITICS AND GOVERNMENT

Praeger Publishers   New York   Washington   London

Library of Congress Cataloging in Publication Data

Wilcox, Dennis L
    Mass media in Black Africa

    (Praeger special studies in international politics
and government)
    Bibliography: p.
    Includes index.
    1. Mass media—Africa, Sub-Saharan. I. Title.
P92.A4W5   301.16'1'096   74-30713
ISBN 0-275-05990-1

PRAEGER PUBLISHERS
111 Fourth Avenue, New York, N.Y. 10003, U.S.A.

Published in the United States of America in 1975
by Praeger Publishers, Inc.

This volume is a descriptive, comparative survey of press-government relationships in independent black Africa, that is, those 34 nations south of the Sahara with black majority governments.

North Africa is excluded not only on geographical and racial grounds but primarily because most scholars, and certainly most of the existing literature, accept the concept of two Africas. One is the Mediterranean Africa with its historic links to the Middle East and the Muslim world. The other Africa, especially further south of the Sahara, has been molded by somewhat different social, political, and cultural influences.

Also excluded from the focus of this text are the areas in black Africa still under the domination of colonial or white minority governments at the time of this research in early 1974. The tiny French territory of Affars and Issas on the Eastern Horn fits into this category as well as the former Portuguese colonies of Angola, Mozambique, and Guinea-Bissau.

Rhodesia (still considered an illegal state by most world nations) and the Republic of South Africa as well as Namibia (Southwest Africa) also are excluded. In the case of Namibia, South Africa still administers the area despite continual UN resolutions ending its mandate. In December, 1974, for example, the UN Security Council adopted a resolution calling on South Africa to withdraw from Namibia by May 30, 1975. South Africa, on the other hand, has shown little interest in obeying the resolution.

This is not to say that the above territories and nations are not an important part of the African setting, but they still have press systems that are essentially European appendages. Consequently, it is difficult to compare them with the indigenous press institutions found in the black-ruled nations that have achieved independence in the past two decades. Since the black nations are now in the overwhelming majority on the continent, the concentration on independent black Africa appears to have a more lasting value.

It also should be said that this volume is not just another recitation of Africa's economic and social shortcomings according to indexes established by Western nations. The chronicle of deficiencies already is well documented to the point of becoming a tired cliché. It is commonly estimated, for example, that about 80 percent of the people in Africa are still functionally illiterate. Fifteen of the nations in black Africa also have the dubious distinction of being amount the 25 poorest countries in the world on the basis of income per capita, industrial production, and literacy. Seven out of ten people still live directly off the land by cultivating the soil or grazing animals.

In terms of mass media, the paucity of the press is only exceeded by the mammoth contrast between the urban and rural areas. In Dakar or Abidjan, today's Paris editions are displayed on well-supplied newsstands that often reach 50 feet in length. Yet it takes a newspaper two or three days to travel from Abidjan to towns in the northern part of the country, 350 miles away. In Dakar, thousands watch television while a village 75 miles away is lucky to have a radio receiver or a newspaper among 350 people. In several countries, the one and only daily newspaper for an entire nation is still printed on an old flatbed press or mimeograph machine.

Yet the press of independent black Africa is worth research and study, not because of its underdevelopment by Western standards, but because the press is an institution that reflects and guages the entire social and political structure of a nation. In many ways, the press is a barometer of a nation's values and socioeconomic life.

Using the press as just one index in independent Africa can be potentially valuable for insight and understanding as the continent gains growing influence in world affairs. These nations comprise more than one-fourth of the United Nations membership and, when voting as a bloc, they exercise formidable influence. Officially these nations only speak for 241 million Africans, but tney dominate the continent and their presence already is part of the world consciousness.

Within this context, however, many often lose sight of the fact that independent black Africa consists of 34 individual and separate nations. All too often, there is the tendency in the United States and Europe to think of Africa as a single, monolithic country with an unstable, authoritarian government. In such a setting, press freedom is written off as an impossibility. Such superficial impressions, of course, are far from the truth. The social, political, and press institutions at work in every country are as diverse as the geography and peoples of Africa.

This volume, then is an attempt to replace impressionistic conceptualizations and isolated incidents concerning the African press with a systematic analysis of the formalized press controls exerted by the individual governments. In this way, the evolving press philosophies of the continent can be better discerned and the pervasiveness of governmental press restraints on a comparative basis can be more accurately determined.

Such a survey is done with the objective of trying to understand the function and role of the press on the African continent, not to judge or condemn it on the basis of comparison with the American or Western European press. Any press, as a societal institution, reflects the values of a given society and only has utility if it fulfills the people's perceived needs. It is only on this basis that the press of Africa should be evaluated and judged.

I wish to acknowledge the encouragement and assistance of many people, both here and abroad, who made this book possible. They include scholars of the African press, UNESCO consultants, officials of the African embassies in Washington, D.C., and employees of the United States Information Agency (USIA). In addition, I am grateful to the several hundred African journalists, foreign correspondents, and government officials who took the time to return a mail questionnaire in early 1974. Many will be mentioned in the footnotes or the bibliography, but others who were equally helpful will be unlisted because of their expressed wish for anonymity.

Dr. Ralph L. Lowenstein, professor of journalism at the University of Missouri, deserves a special mention because he has served as adviser and confidant since this volume was first conceived. My wife, Marianne, is cited for her continuing encouragement and for the countless hours she spent tabulating data. I also wish to thank the journalists, educators, and government information officials who provided me with information and insight during my two visits to East and West Africa in 1971.

I, of course, assume full responsibility for the contents of this project and any errors of fact or judgment should only reflect upon me. It should be pointed out that the bulk of the research was completed before the full military takeover of Ethiopia in the fall of 1974. Consequently, material about the Ethiopian press primarily reflects the situation before Haile Selassie was removed from the throne.

George H. T. Kimble once wrote, "The darkest thing about Africa has always been our ignorance of it." It is hoped that this ignorance about the press in Africa is somewhat dissipated by the following pages.

CONTENTS

LIST OF TABLES AND MAP

Mass Media in
Black Africa

PROFILE OF PRESS CONTROLS
IN INDEPENDENT BLACK AFRICA

The nature of press-government relationships in Africa today is, in large part, due to the legacy left by colonial adminstrators and governments. B. Malinowski has written, "the whole range of European influences, interests, good intentions and predatory drives must become an essential part of the study of African cultural change."[1]

Unfortunately, the tendency in Africa is to ignore the fact that the continent was ever under European domination. African nationalist leaders would like to blot out the colonial experience from their history as if it had never happened. To many of these leaders, the colonial past should be forgotten like a bad dream.

Yet one cannot take this approach if interested in understanding the nature of the contemporary African press and the controls exerted upon it. For, as one writer has correctly summarized,

> the genesis of African journalism lay in dry official publications of colonial governments. The press in Africa began with the publications owned and/or operated by officials of the British government. It began in Sierra Leone in 1801 with the publication of the Royal Gazette. Twenty-one years later, Ghana (then the Gold Coast) followed Sierra Leone's example with the publication of the Royal Gold Coast Gazette.[2]

The same was true in East Africa. Ali Mazrui, one of Uganda's most gifted scholars, said, "It is not for nothing that the word for newspaper in Swahili is 'gazeti.' . . . The Adam and Eve of newspapers in Africa were government gazettes."[3]

In Zambia, for example, the first government-owned newspaper was introduced by the British administration before World War I. And in neighboring Tanganyika (now Tanzania), there were 28 government-operated newspapers during the height of the British involvement.[4] These newspapers, and others like them throughout Africa, were

TABLE 1.1

European Colonial Administration at Independence

European Power	African Colonies
Belgium	Burundi, Rwanda, Zaïre
France	Cameroon,[a] Central African Republic, Chad, Congo, (Brazzaville), Dahomey, Gabon, Guinea, Ivory Coast, Mali, Mauritania, Niger, Senegal, Togo, Upper Volta
United Kingdom	Botswana, Gambia, Ghana, Kenya, Lesotho, Malawi, Nigeria, Sierra Leone, Somalia,[b] Sudan, Swaziland, Tanzania, Uganda, Zambia
Spain	Equatorial Guinea
No colonial legacy	Ethiopia, Liberia

[a]Western Cameroon was under British administration.
[b]Somalia was formed in 1960, joining British and Italian Somaliland.

officially used by colonial officials to promote mass literacy, rural development, and perhaps more important, to counter nationalist activity.

The colonial press, however, was primarily a vehicle for providing news and information to the European population of businessmen and civil servants. Perhaps Jawaharlal Nehru best conveys the imagery of the colonial press in Africa and elsewhere in the British Empire in recalling his youth in India:

I remember that when I was a boy the British-owned newspapers in India were full of official news and utterances; of service news, transfers, and promotions; of the doings of English society, of polo, races, dances, and amateur theatricals. There was hardly a word about the people of India, about their political, cultural, social, or economic life. Reading them, one would hardly suspect that they existed. [5]

The colonial press, as Nehru points out, was ethnocentric in conception and content. One Nigerian journalist bitterly complained that the British press was for the British and the French radio was for the French. He continued, "Both press and radio supported colonial rule and interests and were unsympathetic or outright hostile to African aspirations."[6] In Kenya, for example, the press was somewhat parochial and based mainly on English settler life. The concept of news was information from and about Britain. Even the reporters tended to be drawn from British provincial newspapers, and there was little coverage of African events.

The press in the Belgian Congo was much the same. Papers dealt only with issues and news directly relating to Belgian expatriates. In 1944, for example, the Courrier d'Afrique had all kinds of foreign news but only one column on African affairs. One observer noted, "Information directed toward the African population was almost completely monopolized by the colonial government, and . . . propaganda emphasized the positive aspects of colonial rule and African welfare."[7]

French-dominated Africa provides other examples. What local newspapers existed were generally owned and written by Frenchmen, mainly for Frenchmen. In Mali, for example, the French operated the radio services and most of the programming was in French and aimed at the colonial population. Programming, for the most part, offered only French news and entertainment without much consideration of the interests and needs of the African population.[8]

This preponderance of European content and programming in the mass media was not simply oversight or naivete on the part of the colonial adminstration. Since most literates and people owning radios were Europeans, it was only natural to offer content that would interest them. Africans were a target audience only in an indirect way. In the colonial mind, the essentially European press was a good media for furthering African acculturation to European models in style, dress, speech, tastes, and social norms. James S. Coleman wrote:

> During the period of stabilized colonial rule, the key structure in the socialization process—schools, religious organizations, media of communication, and governmental institutions—were concerned in various ways with rationalizing, perpetuating, and fostering loyalty or conformity to the colonial regime. [Italics added.][9]

Racine Kane, director general of Radio Mali in 1964, agrees. He said, "It was an instrument of the colonizer which served to propogate his culture and to pass words of his policy of domination."[10] And Zambian journalist Kelvin C. Mlenga wrote that the colonial press "tended to work for the preservation of the political status quo and, as a corollary, to frustrate the indigenous people's march to majority rule."[11]

The government-owned and operated press may have dominated the scene in Africa,[12] but there also were newspapers operated by European expatriates independent of the government. There were even newspapers started by Africans. These publications, however, were generally frowned upon and actively discouraged by the colonial officials. In their minds, the majority of African people were barbaric and excitable. A diversity of opinion or misinformation in the press could mislead or inflame the people and threaten the whole basis of colonial power.

One African scholar, searching back into the colonial past, wrote, "Although Britain believed in government by discussion for herself, and was inclined to assume that liberty of though and speech were of universal validity, in governing other peoples outside her homeland she was inevitably autocratic."[13] In 1862, for example, the governor of Nigeria said press liberty was a "dangerous instrument in the hands of semi-civilized Negroes."[14]

Such attitudes by colonial officials continued into the middle of the twentieth century without much change. In 1909, for example, the Seditious Offenses Bill was introduced in Nigeria. Its purpose, according to the Secretary of State, was:

Power . . . to punish publications . . . designed to inflame an excitable and ignorant populace the bulk of whom are absolutely under the control of Headmen and Chiefs who themselves have only recently emerged from barbarism and are still actuated by the old traditions of their race. [15]

French colonial officials also did their best to discourgae an indigenous press. The lieutenant governor of Dahomey wrote a confidential circular in 1933 with the following conclusions:

Most of the papers that appear in Dahomey are incorrectly written, badly edited, the material poorly presented, tendentious, and clearly hostile to the Administration and to the French influence . . . . Without having a precise political doctrine, they show sympathy for certain extreme forms of Communism; their obvious but unacknowledged aim is to prepare for the emancipation of Dahomey by shaking off the yoke of the French. The newspapers of this country support agitators, provoke indiscipline, encourage resistance to the tax, and teach contempt for the authorities. [16]

In Kenya, the rising nationalist aspirations of the native press also were a cause of worry. A communiqué by a government commissioner to the deputy chief secretary of the colony in 1947 noted, "an equally serious cause [of unrest] is the continuous stream of lies, misrepresentations, and colour consciousness which is pouring out from the vernacular presses."[17]

COLONIAL CONTROLS ON THE PRESS

It is obvious that the colonial adminstrators thought a press of any kind was dangerous in the hands of "barbaric" Africans and a critical nationalist press was particularly dangerous. Consequently, colonial governors used their power to punish newspapers that practiced a watchdog role in relation to government. This, of course, included the commercial press operated by expatriates who had the idea that their presses should operate with the same degree of freedom then found in Europe.

William Hachten explained, "Before independence, the daily newspapers were mostly controlled and run by Europeans, and were subjected to harsh and often arbitrary controls by colonial officials."[18] Colin Legum added, "All the colonial governments, without exception, maintained severe forms of censorship, either directly, as in Francophone countries, or indirectly through sedition and other laws."[19]

In the French territories, for example, the establishment of an indigenous press, by either Africans or Europeans, was highly discouraged. One method of discouragement was a heavy tax on the import of newsprint and printing machinery into the African colonies. But there was no import tax on Paris newspapers, so local newspaper production was penalized and the circulation of French newspapers was encouraged.[20] In the French view, this was perfectly consistent with the policy of educating only a few literates and with direct rule from France.

The French colonial policy also forbade anyone except French citizens in good standing to start newspapers and journals in the African territories.[21] This policy was in force until the mid-1930s, and the press development of Francophone Africa still lags behind that of former British West Africa, which tended to have a more liberal policy toward the vernacular press. The Belgian Congo also had a series of governmental ordinances that restricted growth of the press. In 1922, for example, a government decree made the publication and distribution of any journal subject to official permission.[22] This policy was maintained until Congo-Kinshasa (now Zaïre) received its independence in 1960.

Some territories were more fortunate than others. In British West Africa, particularly the nations of Ghana and Nigeria, it is generally believed that the British held a somewhat libertarian view of the press. Native newspapers often were allowed vigorous, sometimes strident, criticism of colonial policies.

Several reasons are advanced for this view. One involves the age of the indigenous press in Nigeria. The Reverend Henry Townsend started Iwe Irohin (The Newspaper) in 1859. Although he was a missionary from the Church Missionary Society in London, the newspaper was the first in Nigeria, published fortnightly in English and Yoruba. Indeed, the missionaries probably gave the native African his first chance to read a newspaper primarily designed for him. Thus, through the

missionary press, the idea of independent newspapers was sown in
British West Africa at an early date.

Second, it is suggested that the British never seriously thought
about settling in West Africa and were primarily concerned with establishing trade bases, not political domination. Consequently, the
British remained on the coastal areas and left the interior to whatever
inroads the missionaries could make. It was somewhat different in
East Africa, where many Englishmen came to garner a little bit of England in the Kenya highlands. These settlers took a proprietary interest
in the land and set about making it their permanent home. Indeed, it
is the settlers who fought the concept of nationalism in East Africa and,
to this day, still resolutely rule Rhodesia despite world censure. In
such a setting, it became important to restrict the indigenous press
and stifle any criticism of government policy.

But one should not be misled into thinking that British West Africa
provided extensive press freedom to the native and expatriate press.
O. S. Coker, a Nigerian journalist of long standing, wrote, "it was a
very strong-handed administration, with you-cannot-do-anything-that-
the-governor-does-not-approve-of philosophy." He continued:

> Within the law of the country the newspaper is allowed to
> say only so much and at the time of colonial rule, that much
> was very little. The "much" you can say was very little
> indeed because the courts were manned by the colonial masters.
> We had very few Nigerian lawyers who could defend us if we
> got into scrapes. The jails were always there and the authority
> of the consul was absolute. So there was very little criticism
> of the government. [23]

Coker's comment about the authority of the consul is well taken
and indicates the crux of the colonial press situation. The British
government never did lay down any clear principles to guarantee the
freedom of the press in the colonies or to govern the press attitudes of
local colonial officials throughout the Empire. As a result, suppression
or liberalization of the press often depended on the local officials'
inclination.

Many of these colonial officials continually sought to control the
newspapers by initiating prosecutions for seditious libel. They also
proposed or passed restrictive laws based on adaptations of obsolete
eighteenth-century laws in England.

Such a mentality is illustrated by Lieutenant Colonel Stephen Hill,
a retired military man who became governor of Sierra Leone in 1855.
He immediately took steps to suppress the outspokenness of Era,
started that same year. He accused the paper of improper and provo-
cative action by commenting adversely on some of his policies. Hill
drew upon antiquated and repressive English press laws to suppress
Era. He posted an ordinance that made it punishable to publish a

newspaper until a signed declaration specifying the names and addresses of the printers, publishers, and owners had been delivered to the register general. In addition, each newspaper was required to post a bond with the governor's office, along with guarantees in the same amount by individuals.

In Hill's mind, such legislation was needed because the Era was in the hands of a few irresponsible Europeans who had an ax to grind. Their ax, he said, was

> to excite to discontent the native population, in which evil cause they may succeed, as it is hardly to be expected that a semi-civilized people easily led by the discontented few, can clearly understand why their government allows the publication of slanderous attacks on its policy and intentions upon them. [24]

The governor's attempt to restrict the press, however, was short-lived. The Colonial Office in London, on hearing about the ordinance, ordered it suspended because it was overly repressive.

Such attempts to restrict the press took place throughout England's colonial empire in Africa. In 1893, a press ordinance was introduced in the Gold Coast (now Ghana) after the Gold Coast People published an article about the colonial judiciary that said, among other things, that the judges took their seats in court three-quarters "tipsy." [25]

The provisions of this ordinance were based on an 1881 press law in England. It provided that the newspaper must submit to the government the names of its owners and pertinent information about them. Printers also were required to place their names on the first and last page of the newspaper.

In 1906, the Kenya Colony also passed an ordinance calling for official registration of newspapers. [26] Nigeria had a seditious offenses bill in 1909 providing that a newspaper could not publish anything that would excite hatred toward the queen of England and the colonial administration. The press also could not publish anything that might cause any official to disregard or fail in his duty. [27] Obviously, such laws could be broadly interpreted if necessary.

The legendary Lord Lugard, governor of Nigeria and architect of Britain's overall policy of indirect rule, also had strong feelings about the press. He thought native newsmen were "mission-educated young men who live in villages interfering with native councils and acting as correspondents for a mendacious native press." [28] His solution was a 1917 law that gave him the right to appoint a newspaper censor whenever an emergency affecting the public safety arose or was about to arise. The law also gave him the power to seize printing facilities or confiscate papers and impose a bond of about $620 on would-be publishers.

The Colonial Office took a dim view of Lugard's solution and ordered him not to enforce such arbitrary rules. Since the Colonial

.Office was thousands of miles away in London, Lord Lugard managed to ignore this dictate and others for various periods of time.

Years later, in 1950, the colonial adminstration banned the Accra Evening News and arrested its editors for sedition. The paper, started by the Convention People's Party, was a major vehicle for nationalist thought. [29] In East Africa, the charge was not sedition but libel. Julius Nyerere, then editor of his political party's newspaper, was prosecuted for criminal libel as a result of comments about bias and discrimination by several district colonial officers. He was found guilty and fined. It is interesting that these same laws were carried over when Nyerere became president of Tanzania. [30]

Direct censorship also was utilized by the colonial governments. In Northern Rhodesia (now Zambia), for example, the Native Film Censorship Board screened all movies that would be seen by Africans. A partial list of criteria for removing scenes included: (1) showing women of easy virtue, (2) prolonged embraces, (3) capture and tying up of Europeans by natives, including North America Indians, (4) deliberate murder at close range, (5) all scenes of obvious crimes, (6) rioting or insurrection scenes, and (7) political demonstrations. [31] It is reported that the government of Rhodesia today continues to practice censorship of movies along these lines.

There were other colonial controls on the press. In Ghana, the criminal code allowed the governor to prohibit importation into the Gold Coast of any newspaper, book, or document he felt was contrary to the public interest. [32] In Tanzania, the governor had the power to prohibit any matter thought to be contrary to the public interest, and news in Swahili (the main lingua franca) was provided for most of the British period by the government's own public relations department. [33]

The posting of bonds was a popular method of press control. In Kenya, the Books and Newspaper Law required all publishers and printers to post a bond of 500 pounds against "libel and seditious activity."[34] Such a large bond, of course, kept the number of newspapers down because only a few people had the financial resources to risk that much money on printing something that might offend the government. The Sudan also required registration and posting of bond. The government, using this method, could suspend the license at any time the governor believed that the newspaper's continued publication was contrary to the interest of public security. [35]

Perhaps the most widespread censorship of the press by the colonial authorities was in Kenya at the start of the Mau Mau uprising. In October 1952, a state of emergency was proclaimed and the government closed nearly 50 African newspapers—almost the entire vernacular press. The way for this action was paved in 1950 when the penal code was amended to give courts power to confiscate any press believed used in the printing of a seditious document that threatened the peace and good order of the colony. The newspapers affected remained suspended throughout the 1950s.

This major incident led one scholar of the African press to point out the paradoxical double standard that existed in colonial press freedom. Joseph Healey, who became a journalist with the religious press in East Africa, once wrote, "In England, the press was governed by common law. In Kenya, press control fell under statutes which afforded local authorities a wide margin of interpretation. This was evident especially in the colonial press laws governing sedition."[36]

The idea that England and its colonies were under the same laws is good in theory, but it was never totally true in reality.

THE RISE OF THE NATIONALIST PRESS

The somewhat oppressive colonial press laws, coupled with the existence of a press primarily operated by Europeans, convinced many Africans that it was highly important to have their own press to reflect their own opinions and desires. For many educated Africans, the colonial press was merely an agent of alienation. Sociologist James Coleman wrote that the colonial press kept "reminding the educated African daily of his subordinate role and confirming in his mind the hopelessness of his political future."[37]

It is in this setting that African nationalism emerged to challenge, compete with, and ultimately displace the colonial institutions in the socialization process. One major vehicle for accomplishing this was the creation of a native press. It was the instrument to get "mental emancipation" from servile colonial mentality, said Nnamdi Azikiwe, an ardent nationalist who is perhaps best known as the publisher of the West African Pilot, a newspaper that played a major role in the rise of Nigerian nationalism. Azikiwe once wrote, "The most potent instrument used in the propagation of nationalist ideas and racial consciousness has been the African-owned nationalist press."[38]

Another Nigerian journalist said, "The indigenous press . . . has invariably served as a rallying point and inspiration to the freedom movement. To the masses, stirring to rid themselves of the shackles of colonialism, this vigorous, militant force with a traditionally anti-government bias has been a source of much encouragement and pride."[39]

In Kenya, for example, the Kikuyu press had about 40 newssheets before the state of emergency closed most of them down. These newssheets were the heart of the nationalist communication system in that colony. Coleman commented, "The rapid development of a communication network among the Kikuyu was one of the critical factors in the nationalist build-up eventuating in the Mau Mau movement."[40]

This role of the press in political communication is perhaps the first and most lasting lesson that aspiring African leaders learned. In both East and West Africa, native newspapers developed as organs of individual political leaders, like Nnamdi Azikiwe, and the political

parties they led. In many cases, political broadsheets were the nationalist movement; organization of political groups with regular membership
lists came at a later date. In the words of James Coleman:

> During the period 1948-1951, the National Council of
> Nigeria and the Cameroons, then the leading nationalist
> organization in Nigeria, existed only in the pages of Nnamdi
> Azikiwe's chain of newspapers; organizationally it was mori-
> bund. The continuity of the press agitation helped to compen-
> sate for the discontinuities in organizational development. [41]

It is interesting to note the number of national leaders in Africa
who began their political careers as editors and publishers of nationalist newssheets. In Kenya, for example, a young man by the name of
Johnstone Kamau started a monthly in Kikuyu during the late 1920s.
Called Muiguithania (meaning Work and Prayer or Bringer of Concord,
depending on the translator), it was published as the official organ of
the Kenya Central Association. That young man, the first African in
Kenya to edit a newspaper, later became known as Jomo Kenyatta.

In neighboring Tanzania, Julius Nyerere began his public career
as editor of Sauti ya TANU before independence. As editor, he was
solidly identified with the nationalist aspirations of his countrymen
and became the country's first president.

Congo-Kinshasa provides other examples. During the 1950s,
President Joseph Motutu of what is now Zaire worked as a journalist.
After independence, Premier Patrice Lumumba gained a major following
by serving as editor of Independence, a journal of opinion. That political and editorial clout helped the nation erupt into chaos during 1960
and ultimately led to Lumumba's death as a martyr to "neocolonialism."

In West Africa, as previously noted, Nnamdi Azikiwe started the
West African Pilot in 1937 for nationalist purposes. He went on to
establish other nationalist newspapers and was a major leader in the
independence movement. After independence, he served Nigeria as
president and governor-general until the military coup of 1966.

As early as 1947, Kwame Nkrumah and the Convention People's
Party (CPP) had started a daily newspaper, the Accra Evening News,
which was banned on several occasions. Nkrumah used the newspaper
as an instrument for mobilizing political support, which eventually
led to independence in 1957. In his autobiography, he wrote, "I
failed to see how any liberation movement could possibly succeed
without an effective means of broadcasting its policy to the rank and
file of the people."[42]

Leopold Sedar-Senghor, president of Senegal, was editor and
publisher of La Condition Humanine in Dakar during the 1950s and used
the publication as the mouthpiece of his evolving political party, the
Senegalese Progressist Party, now formally recognized in the constitution as the only legitimate party in the country. In neighboring Ivory

Coast, President Felix Houphouët-Boigny was the editor of Afrique Noire prior to independence.

Aspiring political leaders elsewhere in French West Africa also considered the press an essential instrument in their cause. In Dahomey, the founders of the first newspapers also were prominent in the agitation for political change and independence. These educated elites were editors in the 1930s but they became the political leaders in the 1940s when nationalist political institutions were formed. [43]

The first indigenous newspaper in Gabon, Echo Gabonais, was founded by leaders of the Jeune Gabonais political party after World War I. When first organized in Guinea, the Parti Démocratique de Guinée (PDG) made early efforts to arouse mass support through a party newspaper, La Liberté. Started in 1950, it was heavily restricted by the colonial authorities and lack of funds, two perennial problems for most of the nationalist press in Africa prior to independence.

Thus, it can readily be seen that the first truly African newspapers were utilized for nationalist purposes and political organization. Although this situation is not unique to Africa, [44] William Hachten makes the Afrian setting clear in the following analysis:

> Historically, the political function of the news media has been of crucial importance in their evolution. The European settlers and colonial officials used their own newspapers and radio stations to reinforce and support their political objectives. The indigenous African press, built on European models, evolved as a political instrument, an organizational tool for molding a political organization, and in time, played a role in the struggle for independence. [45]

Ali Mazrui attributes the historical evolution of the African press to the passion for unity that now affects the content of newspapers in many African states. He said, "The African press was from the start directed toward the attainment of collective goals. The theme of collectivity is what later led to a theme of unity as a goal to be promoted by the press."[46] This theme of unity often precludes the use of the press in Africa today as a source of diverse viewpoints about national issues and problems.

The tradition of a nationalist press also has affected the nature of reporting on the African continent. African journalists generally are uninterested in digging for facts or finding out all the pertinent details. It is not in their tradition because, during the colonial period, indigenous journalism was polemical. Edward Shils commented, "Journalism in colonial countries was the service of a higher cause, not a profession or a business, and the journalism of the underdeveloped countries bears that mark today."[47]

However, it should be noted that this is slowly changing, particularly in Anglophone Africa, as today's journalists are being trained abroad or exposed to

Western libertarian concepts of the press through short courses in their own countries.

But it is the theme of protest, not of news and information, that has shaped the African press to date. Rosalynde Ainslie also noted, "In many countries, the press is descended not from the metropolitan information tradition but from a propagandist past in the days of the anticolonial struggle."[48]

The colonial legacy also has shaped the attitudes of today's African leaders. Many of them, especially those who used the press to garner political power, fear the press because they are familiar with its potential for changing current ruling elites. After independence, many of these leaders expanded their control over the press, not only to keep themselves in power but to integrate mass communications into the important task of national development.

THE CONTINUING COLONIAL LEGACY

To many observers, then, the takeover and control of the press by the new African leaders did not vary considerably from the format and pattern of the colonial press. Colonial press procedures, the subject of scathing criticism before independence, were followed without second thought in many of the post-independence African states.

One area of continuing policy involved ownership. Where once the colonial governments operated and owned much of the communications media, the new African governments assumed the same posture. Colin Legum wrote:

> After independence, television was operated on the same basis as radio—it was wholly owned and controlled by the government, usually under the direct authority of the ministry of information or a commission . . . under ministry supervision.
> The case was the same with the news service. Those that existed before independence were under the direct control of the colonial government; this practice has been continued. In most countries, contracts have been entered into by the government with one or more international agencies for the local distribution of news by radio, television, or the press. But the selection and distribution of items from these external services are controlled by government appointees.[49]

It is charged that in some African countries no real attempt was made to decolonize the Western model of communication or to integrate the traditional African culture into more effective communications for the masses. The ruling African elites, educated in Britain or France, continued to use the mass media for their own edification. In French

West Africa, for example, the press is still criticized for only addressing itself to the more sophisticated town dweller with sufficient education to grasp discussions of political and economic issues. There also are strong links between the African elites and the former colonial power. When Senghor of Senegal gives a press conference, for example, it is customary that only French journalists can ask questions.[50]

A Nigerian journalist and educator has written, "What was apparent was a change of name and ownership in some cases. The post-colonial newspapers, radio and television still talk with a minority in the same format, the same content, the same style as in the colonial era."[51]

Another manifestation of elitism is in the language used for mass communications. In some Francophone nations, as in Ivory Coast, most radio broadcasting was in French, a language used by less than 10 percent of the population. It is only in recent years that some African nations have tried to diversify their mass media by using the major indigenous languages and dialects. Mauritania, for example, now prints its daily news bulleting in French and Arabic. Tiny Rwanda has a weekly in Kinyarwanda, the major language of the country, and Ethiopa has dailies in Amharic.

The mass media of the Ivory Coast well illustrate the continuing colonial model. The press is still dominated by the government and independence merely meant a change of ownership and personalities. Admittedly, the people of the country probably accept this form of governmental control because it is all they have known since becoming a French colony in 1895.

It is in this context that William Hachten has suggested that the need for an independent press may never have crossed the people's minds. He wrote, "A free press has never been known; negative criticism was considered irresponsible, and articulate critics were usually absorbed by the establishment of the president. If not, they left the country."[52]

The ruling African elites also express a degree of paternalism toward their follow Africans when it comes to having an unbridled press. Many African leaders, just like the colonial civil servants, do not think the African masses could handle free discussion. French-educated Laurent Dona-Fologo, the extremely capable editor of the daily Fraternite-Matin said, "In underdeveloped countries there is never total liberty—the people are still too susceptible and emotional and don't have lucid judgments. So we don't give them everything."[53]

Journalist and author Timothy Green, in surveying African broadcasting, also discussed the African rationale for controlling television content:

> The usual justification for it is exactly the same as that given for not allowing violence, namely that the people are totally unsophisticated: they believe everything they see on the box, so it is much the best that they see a nice government line and nothing else.[54]

The colonial legacy also continues in press laws left over from the colonial period. In Kenya, for example, the libel laws are based on English law prior to 1956. Since that time Britain has amended its libel laws to make it more difficult to prove libel, but these amendments were never made in Kenya and it is still unnecessary to prove damage in libel cases. [55]

In Francophone Africa, the same situation exists. Most nations have kept French legal and penal codes although many laws have been wiped off the books in France. Consequently, in Africa one can still be fined or imprisoned for defamation of the courts, army, public authorities, and the administration. Periodic censorship also is not uncommon, presumably sanctioned by law left over from the French administration when news was carefully controlled. [56]

And finally, the colonial legacy is still evident in the extensive network of government information services operated by most African states. James Coleman has provided insight on this issue:

> At the height of agitational politics, when colonial governments were subject to unrelenting invective by the nationalist press, the British government gave high priority to the development of public relations departments specifically charged with the task of explaining government policies and programs for the masses. This engendered intense competition between nationalist propagandists and colonial governments, which led to a progressive widening and deepening of the communication process.
>
> When nationalists finally approached the threshold of political power they were determined that one of their first acts would be the dissolution of all government public relations activities. Once in power, however, they saw the utility of the official apparatus of mass communication which had been developed during colonialism, particularly as they became increasingly impressed with the difficulties in realizing their ambitious programs and the consequent need to rationalize and explain postponement or nonfulfillment. The result is that public relations departments acquired a new lease on life, and had their activities expanded. [57]

Thus, by examining the colonial antecedents of the press, it is hoped that one can better understand the forces that shaped the contemporary African press scene.

It is only natural that African leaders, once they assumed political power, continued to follow many aspects of the colonial press since that was the only model they knew. Control of the press made sense, not only from the standpoint of their own security but for utilization in programs of national development.

But the question remains, whether the African nations, one or two decades into independence, will continue to fall back on colonial models.

There is now a great movement to Africanize the social, economic, and cultural institutions inherited from the colonial past. Many African leaders are now convinced that European models of development do not quite fit the unique problems of Africa or take into account its traditional culture. In this context, new press philosophies are also evolving to fit the African experience.

One also must ask, what types of press controls are now being exerted in Africa and how they are different from the colonial models. Ali Mazrui wrote:

> The question which now arises is whether newspapers in independent Africa are about to resume their earliest role in the history of colonialism—and become government gazettes, or "magazeti ya serikali" all over again. In at least some African countries what were once vigorous newspapers have indeed been reduced to official gazettes or government bulletins. In other African countries a similar possiblity is clearly visible. It is felt by many African leaders that the journalistic freedom which had helped to create African nationalism could not be trusted to create African nationhood. Relative freedom of the press helped to achieve independence; but it could not be relied upon to achieve national integration after independence. Or so the argument goes. [58]

Indeed, Mazrui has a legitimate question, one worth exploring.

NOTES

1. B. Malinowski, "The Dynamics of Social Change," in Social Change: The Colonial Situation, ed. Emmanuel Wallerstein (New York: John Wiley and Sons, 1966), p. 11.

2. John N. Williams, "The Press and Printed Word in Africa," Overseas Quarterly, December 1963, p. 243.

3. Ali A. Mazrui, "The Press, Intellectuals and the Printed Word," in Mass Thoughts, eds. Edward Moyo and Susan Rayner (Kampala: Makerere University Press, 1972), p. 162.

4. Titus Mukupo, "What Role for the Government in the Development of an African Press?" Africa Report 11 (January 1966): 40.

5. Jawaharlal Nehru, "The Discovery of India," in Social Change: The Colonial Situation, p. 67.

6. Francis Okwuadigbo Ugboajah, "Traditional-Urban Media Model: Stocktaking for African Development," Gazette, 18, no. 2 (1972): 82.

7. Area Handbook for the Democratic Republic of the Congo (Kinshasa), prepared by the Foreign Area Studies Program of the

American University (Washington, D. C.: U. S. Government Printing Office, 1971), p. 275.

8. Charles Cutter, "Political Communication in a Pre-Literate Society: The Radio in Mali," paper presented to the annual meeting of the African Studies Association in Denver, November 3, 1971, p. 2.

9. James S. Coleman, "The Politics of Sub-Saharan Africa," in The Politics of the Developing Areas, eds. Gabriel A. Almond and James S. Coleman (Princeton, N. J.: Princeton University Press, 1960), p. 334.

10. Cutter, "Political Communication in a Pre-Literate Society," p.2.

11. Kelvin G. Mlenga, "What Sort of Press Freedom?" The Journalist's World 3, no. 2 (1965): 15.

12. Alhaji Babatunde Jose, "The Press in Nigeria," speech presented to the opening session of the Distripress in Athens, Greece, on October 23, 1973. In this speech, the managing director of the Daily Times in Lagos pointed out that a government press was in existence even before the British came to Nigeria. He said, "Long before the British came to Nigeria [the earliest arrivals were merchant seamen followed later in 1843 by Christian missions], the monthly Kano Chronicle, printed in Arabic and Hausa, was published by the Kano Emirate Administration."

13. Fred I. A. Omu, "The Dilemma of Press Freedom in Colonial Africa: The West African Example," Journal of African History 9, no. 2 (1968): 280.

14. Ibid., p. 288.

15. Ibid., p. 293.

16. Dov Ronen, "Political Development in a West African Country: The Case of Dahomey," Ph. D. dissertation, Indiana University, 1969, p. 132. This confidential circular by the lieutenant governor was published in Le Phare du Dahomey; for publishing the circular, the newspaper was banned for three months.

17. F. D. Cornfield, "Historical Survey of the Origins and Growth of Mau Mau" (London: Colonial Office, 1960), p. 191, as cited in Norman N. Miller, "Kenya: Nationalism and the Press 1951-1961," master's thesis, Indiana University, 1962, p. 79.

18. William A. Hachten, "Newspapers in Africa: Change or Decay," Africa Report 15 (December 1970): 25.

19. Colin Legum, "The Mass Media–Institutions of the African Political Systems," in Reporting Africa, ed. Olav Stokke (Uppsala: Scandinavian Institute of African Studies, 1971), p. 29.

20. Rosalynde Ainslie, The Press in Africa: Communications Past and Present (New York: Walker, 1966), p. 130.

21. Area Handbook for Senegal, prepared by the Foreign Area Studies Program of the American University (Washington, D. C.: U. S. Government Printing Office, 1963), p. 278.

22. Ainslie, The Press in Africa, p. 120.

23. O. S. Coker, "Mass Media in Nigeria," in Mass Media Systems, ed. Royal D. Colle for the Department of Communication Arts,

New York State College of Agriculture (Ithaca, N. Y.: Cornell University, 1968), p. 43.

24. Omu, "The Dilemma of Press Freedom in Colonial Africa, " p. 284.

25. Ibid., p. 287.

26. Miller, "Kenya: Nationalism and the Press 1951-1961, " p. 23.

27. Omu, "The Dilemma of Press Freedom in Colonial Africa, " p.293.

28. Ugboajah, "Traditional-Urban Media Model, " p. 83.

29. Jon Woronoff, West African Wager: Houphouet versus Nkrumah (Metuchen, N. J.: Scarecrow Press, 1972), p. 25.

30. Margaret L. Bates, "Tanganyika, " in African One-Party States, ed. Gwendolen Carter (Ithaca, N. Y.: Cornell University Press, 1963), P. 427.

31. Leonard Doob, "Information Services in Central Africa, " Public Opinion Quarterly 17 (Spring 1953): 18.

32. Walter Bunge, "Some Aspects of Press Law in Africa, " paper presented to the Association for Education in Journalism, Berkeley, Calif., 1969, p. 17.

33. Graham L. Mytton, "Tanzania: The Problems of Media Development, " Gazette 14, no. 2 (1968): 99.

34. Joseph Healey, "Press Freedom in Kenya, " Report 191 prepared for the Freedom of Information Center, University of Missouri, 1967, p. 3.

35. Bunge, "Some Aspects of Press Law in Africa, " p. 20.

36. Healey, "Press Freedom in Kenya, " p. 2.

37. Coleman, "The Politics of Sub-Saharan Africa, " p. 347.

38. James S. Coleman, "Nationalism in Tropical Africa, " in Independent Black Africa: The Politics of Freedom, ed. William J. Hanna (Chicago: Rand McNally, 1964), p. 224.

39. Mlenga, "What Sort of Press Freedom, " p. 15.

40. Coleman, "The Politics of Sub-Saharan Africa, " p. 348.

41. Ibid., p. 350.

42. Kwame Nkrumah, The Autobiography of Kwame Nkrumah, p. 76, as cited in Ali Mazrui, "The Press, Intellectuals and the Printed Word, " p. 163.

43. Ronen, "Political Development in a West African Country: The Case of Dahomey, " p. 125.

44. The evolution of the press in Europe and Asia also shows that the press was first used as a form of political communication and partisan comment. The press in Europe and Asia also was highly nationalistic when individual countries were being occupied by foreign powers. For more information on this aspect, see Kenneth E. Olson, The History Makers—The Press in Europe from Its Beginnings Through 1965 (Baton Rouge: Louisiana State University Press, 1966); John A. Lent, ed. Reluctant Revolution (Ames: Iowa State University Press, 1971).

45. William A. Hachten, Muffled Drums (Ames: Iowa State Univeristy Press, 1971), p. 272.

46. Ali A. Mazrui, Cultural Engineering and Nation-Building in East Africa (Evanston, Ill.: Northwestern University Press, 1972), p. 54.

47. Edward Shils, "Intellectuals, Public Opinion and Economic Development, " in Independent Black Africa: The Politics of Freedom, ed. Hanna, p. 483.

48. Ainslie, The Press in Africa, p. 137.

49. Legum, "The Mass Media–Institutions of the Africa Political Systems, " p. 27.

50. Ely J. Kahn, The First Decade: A Report on Independent Black Africa (New York: W. W. Norton, 1972), p. 34.

51. Ugboajah, "Traditional-Urban Media Model, " p. 88.

52. Hachten, Muffled Drums, p. 6.

53. Kahn, The First Decade, p. 34.

54. Timothy Green, The Universal Eye (New York: Stein and Day, 1972), p. 276.

55. Joseph Healey, "Press Freedom in Kenya, " p. 3. The material referred to is a letter from Henry Reuter, a journalist of long experience in East Africa, dated 1966.

56. Area Handbook for Senegal, p. 293.

57. Coleman, "The Politics of Sub-Saharan Africa, " p. 351.

58. Mazrui, "The Press, Intellectuals and the Printed Word, " p. 164.

CHAPTER

2

THE MULTIFACETED
ROLE OF THE PRESS

The colonial legacy certainly influence and shaped the press institutions of black Africa, but today's national leaders are now the prime
decision makers who will decide whether to continue that legacy or
initiate new press-government relationships. Indeed, the role and
responsibilities of the African mass media are highly correlated with
the attitudes and goals of high government officials.

Olav Stokke, associate director of the Scandinavian Institute of
African Affairs, wrote:

> Several factors may influence the degree of control and
> direction of governmental owned newspapers and the non-
> government mass media as well. The most important variable
> in this regard is probably the attitude to the role and functions
> of the mass media prevailing, first of all, within the govern-
> ment but also within the predominant social and political
> environment in general, especially at the elite level. [1]

Thus, it is important to explore the attitudes of the ruling elites
toward the press and their perceptions of the function of the press.
As with nearly everything else in Africa, there is hardly universal
unanimity about the role and responsibilities of the print and electronic
media. Attitudes, even among the same leaders, change with time and
events. Also, the operation of mass media is discussed at two levels,
the idealistic and actual reality.

At the beginning of the decade for independence, a pan-African
committee drafted a somewhat idealistic statement about the role of
the press in emerging independent black Africa. According to its published resolution:

> The function of the press is to inform, to educate, to
> entertain and amuse, to examine fairly and critically and to

make constructive contributions to thought and discussion on
matters of public policy and to provide a forum for the airing
of ideas and opinions, whatever their origin and however
controversial. [2]

For many African journalists trained in Western Europe or the United
States, this resolution seemed highly reasonable and logical. One
Nigerian journalist probably thought it came to describing the press in
his own nation. He wrote, as late as 1968, the following description
of the Nigerian press:

This is the basic philosophy on which our communication
media operate—that no matter what happens, we shall, like
Socrates, seek the truth rather than try to persuade, and this
is what our newspapers, our radio stations, our television
stations and our other media of mass communication try to do;
present the story as it is, with very little color. Human nature
being what it is, you know, occasionally there is some slant
to presentation, but in the main, the policy is to present the
truth. [3]

Such lofty thoughts, even in the West, often do not match reality.
Ideals often are dissipated, and Zambia is a good mini-case study.
President Kenneth Kaunda, at the 1968 annual assembly of the International Press Institute in Nairobi, spent some time discussing the
concept of press freedom. He said, "We recognize the importance of
an independent press completely objective and free from the influence
of government. "[4]

In later months, Kaunda added interpretation to his original statement at IPI, saying, "The government reserves the right to act as arbiter
of this [press] freedom in the interests of defense, and in matters of
public safety, order, morality, health. "[5] By 1972, Kaunda had decided
that the Zambian press would no longer be allowed to "mislead the
masses through misrepresentation or distortion of facts. "[6] The nation's
two dailies, The Daily Mail and the Times of Zambia, are now operated
by editors appointed by the now formalized one-party government, and
"objectivity" is defined by the United Nationalist Independence Party. [7]

This is not surprising. Objectivity, by its very nature, is subjective. In the words of sociologist Herbert Passin:

Where the political temperature is high, the journalist
usually considers "objectivity" and "commitment" to be the
same thing, because both are identified with "the truth"; what
is "true" is naturally "objective" and what he believes is
naturally "true. " This linkage holds whether the journalist
is in opposition, say to a colonial government, or in support
of a movement or government in power. [8]

African leaders also define press freedom somewhat differently.
Julius Nyerere, for example, believes in press freedom only within
a narrow framework. He has compared a new, developing nation to a
country at war–and in wartimes newspapers everywhere accept limitations on their freedom. [9] He has said that an irresponsible press cannot
be allowed to "deflect the government from its responsibilities to the
people by creating problems of law and order."[10]

The only problem with this somewhat typical attitude of African
leaders is their tendency to be both judge and jury of what is in the
national interest. As Hilary B. Ng'weno, an East African journalist of
long and varied experience, wrote:

> Obviously, like all other freedoms, the freedoms that
> newspapers should enjoy in their treatment of newsworthy
> events and comments should be subject to limitations dic-
> tated by the national interest. The trouble is that in most
> countries governments tend to treat themselves as the sole
> judges of what constitutes the national interest. [11]

It is interesting to note that the concept of relative press freedom
varies even between military governments. In Nigeria, for example,
General Yakubu Gowon has set a somewhat liberal tone in explaining
the current status of the Nigerian press:

> I cannot tell them what to do since we do not dictate policy
> to any press here; they have been independent as they ought
> to be. The press has to tell the truth, to be objective and
> honest so that the people can rely on what they print. They
> should tell us off when they feel we are wrong and commend
> when they feel it's worthwhile: We can take it. [12]

In neighboring Ghana, also under military leadership, the tone is
somewhat different. Major A. H. Selormey, commissioner for information, has told the press to tread softly:

> we will allow the freedom of the press to operate in this
> country as far as it is consistent with a military government
> . . . . Every newsman should be experienced enough to know
> that a military regime is not a regular or normal state of
> affairs and that there is a need for caution and circumspection
> in their work. A military government, by its very nature, is
> certainly inconsistent with any pretentions to subscribing
> fully to the concept of freedom of the press in the normal accep-
> tance of the expression. [13]

HARNESSING THE PRESS FOR PROMOTIONAL GOALS

In fact, the emphasis should be not on the restrictive aspects of
the mass media function but on promotional utilization of the press for
the good of government and party. Many observers feel that the primary
role of the press in developing countries, including Africa, is to act as
an arm or instrument of official government policy. A random survey of
African countries seems to document this contention.

In the Congo (formerly Congo-Brazzaville), for example, it is not
uncommon for journalists to attend ideological seminars. During one
such seminar in 1966, it was made clear to the assembled group that
the press was essentially an instrument of the state apparatus. [14] The
rationale for this generalized concept is explained by a Zambian journalist, Titus Mukupo:

> When governments need to explain policy, transmit their
> decisions, instructions, wishes, suggestions, or laws, or
> discuss new projects and ideas with their electorate, they
> must have a forum which is not antagonistic to the overall
> goals of national policy. [15]

Radio Mali serves essentially the same role as a government ampli-
fier. One American scholar said, "The radio was a principal instrument
in the construction of the nation, a principal support of its economic
and cultural policies . . . . Radio Mali pursued these tasks through
a variety of programmes all of which have one thing in common: the
furtherance of party policy. "[16]

A glance at African newspapers also shows a high degree of exhor-
tation and many directives flowing daily from the mass media. According
to one researcher in East Africa,

> much of the exhorting tone is the result of the considerable
> attention given to politicians' speeches which, when simpli-
> fied and summarized, often sound like requests or commands;
> plant more tobacco, drink less pombe, work harder, use
> Swahili, and so forth. [17]

In Tanzania, an editor for a Tanganyika African National Union
(TANU) publication makes no apology for this. He said, "We preach
and exhort about 90 percent of the time. " A comparison of headlines
is instructive. The Standard, before it was nationalized, ran an article
about a government plan to increase the use of Swahili. Its headline
was, "Government Plans Swahili Committee. " In the Nationalist, a
daily operated by TANU, the headline over the same story read, "Boost
Up Swahili. "[18]

In West Africa, various governments also put much stock in the ability of the press to enunciate policy and inspire a following. In Togo, for example, one journalist said, "the press is considered a powerful weapon. That is why it should only pursue one goal: to serve and support decisions of the party or the government in power."[19]

The press also is seen as a revolutionary tool. In such nations as Guinea, the Congo, and Somalia, the mass media are servants of a central revolutionary purpose organized along Marxist lines. Their function is to explain and inspire rather than to criticize or serve as a watchdog on the excesses of government.

In Guinea, for example, the press educates the people about the socialist philosophy and how to work under President Sekou Touré's "scientific socialism."[20] Since the Parti Démocratique de Guinée (PDG) has exclusive control over all aspects of national life, including operation of the country's only daily newspaper, this objective is efficiently carried out.

Perhaps the most explicit and consistent African advocate of the press as a revolutionary instrument was Kwame Nkrumah of Ghana. During his years of national leadership (1957-66), he continually elaborated upon the role of the revolutionary press in Africa and exhorted other African leaders, with some success, to utilize the press in the same way.

In 1963, at a meeting of the Pan-African Union of Journalists in Accra, Nkrumah said:

> Our revolutionary African press must present and carry forward our revolutionary purpose. This is to establish a progressive political and economic system upon our continent that will free men from want and every form of social injustice and enable them to work out their social and cultural destinies in peace and at ease.[21]

And during the dedication of the Ghana News Agency building in 1965, Nkrumah said:

> The necessity for a clear ideology of the African revolution must be to view problems in the right perspective so that they [journalists] can write them with insight and understanding. The drumbeat of the African revolution must throb in the pages of his newspapers and magazines; it must sound in the voices and feelings of our news readers. To this end, we need a new kind of journalist for the African revolution.[22]

Or again:

> The true African journalist very often works for the organ of the political party to which he himself belongs and in whose

purpose he believes. He works to serve a society moving in
the direction of his own aspirations. How many journalists
of the imperialist and neo-colonist press have this satisfaction?[23]

But apparently not all African countries have formulated such suc-
cinct philosophies of the press, and even Ghana has changed considerably since Nkrumah fell from power. Ethiopia, under a monarch,
until recently, is an example of a nation without a specific overall
policy about the press. One observer noted before the military takeover
in 1974·

The newspapers have scarcely been used to inform the
people of political affairs, even to the extent of putting the
government's case; they usually contain little more than a
record of the Emperor's activities, foreign news taken directly
from the agencies, and a few local items of no political signi-
ficance, though exhortatory leading articles have become more
common in the last few years. [24]

In general, there are probably four major attitudes expressed by
African leaders about the role and function of the press in independent
black Africa. These themes are: (1) harnessing the press for nation-
building; (2) the press as an instrument of national unity; (3) the need
for "constructive" criticism; and (4) the press an an agent of mass education.

NATION BUILDING

"All news is designed to assist national development. It begins
and comes back to that, " according to Cire Thiam of Senegal, a delegate
to IPI's second Anglophone-Francophone meeting during 1971 in Cameroon. [25] For him and many other delegates, nation building consists
of creating a national consciousness and unity within a heterogenous
people.

Lloyd Sommerlad, author of The Press in Developing Countries,
agrees. He has said:

They need the press to help create a feeling of nationhood
among people traditionally divided by tribal loyalties; to
explain the objectives of a new socialist society; to spread
information about new and better ways of living and farming;
to obtain cooperation in community and national projects;
to win support for the party and its leadership. [26]

This concept of using the press for nation building, of course, means a high degree of government direction and a corresponding decline in press freedom as defined in the West. Indeed, the rationale for a controlled press is the fact that all segments of society must be mobilized to realize national plans of development.

To some, like Eddie Agyemang, editor of the Mirror in Ghana, Africa needs all the energies of its people for nation building and cannot afford the luxury of encouraging dissident newspapers. [27] Another African journalist, Theodore Magloe of Togo, thinks the freedom of the press should exist only in the context of furthering national development. He said, "After all, the primordial urgency for an underdeveloped country is to develop. That is the essential task."[28]

This theme is expressed by a variety of other African leaders, regardless of political philosophy, and often forms the basis of press-government relationships. In Nigeria, for example, Alhaji Babatunde Jose, chairman of the Daily Times, said:

in the new nations and traditional societies of Africa . . . a journalist has additional responsibilities–to help in building a nation out of the multi-lingual, multi-cultured societies in countries where economic resources are inadequate to meet the expectations of the people . . . . In the final analysis, the journalists are part of the Nigerian society. If a society decays, the journalist cannot claim to be healthier than the body and if law and order breaks down and there is chaos, there would be no newspapers, no journalists and no readers. [29]

In Kenya, President Jomo Kenyatta has said, "The press should positively promote national development and growing self-respect."[30] Further, "The press in Africa can have tremendous influence in nation-building. It may constantly inspire, or could set out to frustrate the spirit of Harambee or national unity which every young country needs as the fundamental of its progress."[31]

Elsewhere in East Africa, leaders look at the process of national development in terms of news content. A. A. Ojera, Uganda minister of information in 1966, said, "perverse criticism is a brake on progress and frustrates the authorities of the people interested in development."[32] In Tanzania, Information Minister Daudi Mwakawago said standards of reporting national development should be upgraded: "To our newsmen, if a leader meets with an accident and is injured, that is more news than if 100 villagers decide to dig a trench to get water they have been doing without for years."[33]

After the 1969 military coup in the Sudan, the ruling Revolutionary Command Council (RCC) took steps to nationalize all privately owned newspapers and news agencies. It acted, according to official statements, because the privately-owned press was distorting government

policy statements and practicing excessive commercialism instead of
participating in nation building. [34]

The action in the Sudan is a direct result of the concept that the
press should participate in nation building. Derek Davies, a writer for
the Far Eastern Economic Review, summarized the dilemma:

> Every time the press acquiesces in the exaggeration of
> the function it plays within society–and particularly within
> developing society–it provides politicians with more ammuni-
> tion against it and with more excuses for bringing it under
> control or censorship. [35]

THE NEED FOR NATIONAL UNITY

A companion theme to the press role in nation building is its function
of creating and maintaining national unity. Tom Mboya, one of Kenya's
outstanding politicians before his assassination, wrote this way about
the relationship between national unity and freedom of the press:

> Because the leaders are trying hard to create unity, they
> become sensitive to anyone who appears to act as though he
> constituted an opposition and did nothing but criticize the
> government's efforts. Freedom of the press in a new country
> has, therefore, got to be limited; not so much restricted by
> legislation, but rather deliberately guided, for its main func-
> tions, include not only giving news, but also taking part in
> the national effort and contributing toward the building of a
> nation. [36]

In the same line, President Kenyatta has said, "the press should
always seek to coalesce, rather than to isolate, the different cultures
and aspirations and standards of advancement which make up our new
nation."[37] Even Kenyan journalists, primarily exposed to British concepts of press freedom, seem to agree with this evaluation. Hilary
Ng'weno thinks the press should first be used to unify the nation against
the influence of intertribal and intercommunal disputes. [38]

This concept of promoting unity is somewhat alien to the Western
world, where freedom is the paramount ethical preference associated
with the press. Freedom of the press in the United States, for example,
is regarded as inseparable from civil liberties.

In Africa, on the other hand, press development did not stem from
the concepts of individual freedom but from the historical background
of national freedom from colonial rule. Thus, the concept of national
unity for overthrowing colonial rule was well integrated into the African

press and remains so today. Since unity is a highly valued concept in Africa, there is a continuing tendency to regard the mass media as instruments of generating national unity in the face of economic adversity. The struggle against colonialism is now the mobilizing of forces against poverty and ignorance. In such a setting, individual freedoms and viewpoints are sacrificed for the greater national good.

According to Ali Mazrui, this need for generating national unity is not totally unfamiliar in the West. During World War II, there was a felt need for national unity in the United States and it was solved primarily by voluntary censorship on the part of the press. Justice Holmes also introduced the concept of "clear and present danger," which serves to regulate freedom of speech and press. Mazrui stated·

> African leaders like Nyerere, the late Tom Mboya and
> others have often asserted that the crisis of underdevelopment
> and the fragility of political institutions together constitute a
> moment of national emergency in no way less critical than that
> confronting the United States in its war effort during the 1940s. [39]

The Kennedy administration managed the news and deceived the press during the Cuban missile crisis, Mazrui said, "because the naked truth could be an enemy to a nation's welfare in times of crisis." For many Africans, this argument seems to make sense because there is a strong possibility of civil strife between ethnic groups in Africa. For them, this is a "clear and present danger."

In 1966, for example, a radio broadcast apparently ignited the second massacre of the Ibo in northern Nigeria. The broadcast, from a neighboring country, reported the killing of Hausa in eastern Nigeria by Ibo. The north retaliated on the basis of the broadcast. [40] When Tom Mboya was killed in 1959, the Voice of Kenya did not report it right away because of fears such a report would incite Luo tribesmen (Mboya's tribe) to retaliate by killing Kikuyu who, it was thought, probably had killed Mboya. [41]

Uganda provides another example, although no violence resulted. In the celebrated suppression of Transition magazine, the editor and a letter writer were jailed in 1969 for criticizing the slow progress in putting Ugandans on the High Court. In the government's view, the letter to the editor constituted a form of tribal incitement because the letter had mentioned tribal considerations as the probable reason for the delay. Such speculation, said the government, could stir up tribal loyalties and destroy national unity.

Despite these considerations, Mazrui apparently thinks the passion for unity and the resulting suppression of differing viewpoints in the press is potentially harmful in the long run. As a conflict theorist, he stated:

there are fundamental fallacies in this whole line of reasoning.
One is the assumption that avoiding conflict is the same thing
as achieving integration. And so African governments often
go to great lengths to avert the appearance of dissention in
the country and to try and eliminate every risk of serious conflict,
either between groups or between the state itself and some
groups. What is overlooked is that there is such a thing as
artificial "absence of conflict." National integration does not
consist merely of our being forced to smile sweetly at each
other.

This then is the first fallacy of those who argue that open
clashes of opinion are harmful to nation-building. They are
wrong in assuming that to avert conflict between groups is the
same thing as to integrate these groups. They forget that the
groups could never be integrated unless risks of conflict are
taken. [42]

"CONSTRUCTIVE" CRITICISM

The third theme of African journalism is the pressure for "constructive" or "responsible" criticism. The term is subject to broad interpretation but generally means that a dim view is taken of any press content
perceived as a negative comment on the performance of a government
official or policy.

In explanation, E. J. B. Rose, former director of the International
Press Institute (IPI), stated:

    The words "constructive criticism" have become a catch
    phrase, a parrot cry of politicians. They really want press and
    radio to concentrate on the positive, confidence-raising aspects
    of the news and play down those negative and sometimes pain-
    ful manifestations of political and social turmoil which should
    be reported. They want editors to applaud what we call "sun-
    shine stories" (there will be a hydro-electric works in five
    years, new universities in three years and so on) and not to
    comment on abuses or shortcomings such as corruption and
    maladminstration. [43]

The other aspect of constructive criticism is the tendency to
regard unfavorable comment as disloyal and damaging to the national
character. In many African countries, criticism of the government is
taken to mean ciriticism of the nation as a whole. As a Ugandan
editor stated,

Particularly in Africa . . . governments try to identify
themselves very closely with the state. This is an intentional
manoeuvre as a method of entrenchment . . . it leads to the
warning; "If you criticize me, (that is, the government) you
are criticizing the state" and then the case is far more serious
for that is almost sedition. [44]

Consequently, newspapers and electronic media are very cautious
in their criticisms. But some attempts are made to give the appearance
of criticism even amoung the government-owned newspapers. In Ivory
Coast, Fraternité-Matin occasionally criticizes the government on such
minor issues as the degree of diligence of post office clerks. As in the
Soviet Union, if a major government official is criticized, it is generally
a sign that a high-level decision has already been reached to dismiss
or demote him.

The plea for constructive criticism, in the minds of African leaders,
does not mean opposition to freedom of the press. In Zambia, Foreign
Minister Simon Kapwepwe once said,

My government upholds the freedom of the press, but I
would add a qualification . . . the editorial columns of our
newspapers, through the spoken word or projected by other
means, should be constructive and responsible. [45]

Liberia has liberalized its press policies since William Tolbert
took office in 1971 after the death of William Tubman. Dr. Edward M.
Kesserly, minister of information, explained the president's new policies as follows:

The president wants to build a new society and he has
called for the total involvement of all the people. We need to
hear what our people are thinking—we will not gag them. Of
course, we would prefer constructive criticism to help us make
national plans. [46]

The concept of constructive criticism is not just a political expe-
dient; it has a basis in traditional African values. Although the Western
world places high value on criticism of government officials as a criterion of press independence, the African framework is different. Most
traditional African cultures have a high respect for authority and it is
considered disrespectful to challenge or gossip about ethnic and now
national leadership. This attitude of respect keeps Kenyan journalists
from giving the age of President Kenyatta (now over 80) or speculating
about successors. [47]

Westerners also are shocked and somewhat amused at the blatant
praise of leaders in the African press, but this also is anchored in

traditional African values. Terms of praise that sound ridiculous to Western ears are a normal aspect of ordinary relations between many chiefs and their followers. This is an integral part of courteous ceremonial ritual which, in some African societies, can go on for hours. [48] Since many Africans conceptualize the press as an instrument of their leaders, it is only natural that the proper protocol of praise should be observed.

MASS EDUCATION

The mass media in Africa also are controlled by government in varying degrees because they are considered a primary instrument of mass education. In countries where there is a lack of capital resources and teachers, a government-owned and operated press is the only way that the masses are exposed to education and socialized into the modern sector.

In Ethiopia, for example, most major newspapers and broadcasting are under the Ministry of Information. One reason advance for this is the official view that the modern mass media are valuable tools in public education. Officials believe that mass communications must be geared to such national needs as education, literacy, industrial development, agricultural reform, and procurement of foreign aid. [49] Such objectives, of course, are governmental in nature rather than major functions of a privately owned press.

Radio is particularly useful for mass education because it capitalizes on Africa's great oral tradition and does not require literacy. Tanzania, for example, utilizes broadcasting for education and to generate active party participation. Radio programs are followed by discussions, local talks, and information pamphlets. Scripts are distributed to district offices before the program so local officers can coordinate activities and provide additional information.

The same is true in Malawi, where an AID team from the University of Missouri assisted in the construction and initial operation of a new radio station serving rural areas. Programming is done in conjunction with the agricultural extension service. This approach helps diffuse innovations and reinforces what the extension agents tell the people. [50]

Theodore Magloe of Togo well summarizes the educational role of the press in Africa as follows:

> The states are interested in the development of the press
> and authorize the necessary advances because they have
> recognized that the press is a mass education medium over
> and above its function of information. [51]

And an American scholar has noted, "Information and education become synonymous in a developing country."[52]

THE AFRICAN PRESS IN PERSPECTIVE

It can be seen that the African media derive their impetus not from the tradition of defending individual civil liberties but from the felt need to harness the press for national liberation and then national integration. The latter is particularly relevant since many diverse groups found themselves in the same nation due to arbitrary boundaries set by the European powers at the Berlin Conference of 1885. In most cases, the criteria in establishing boundaries were geographical and mutually agreed colonial spheres of influence rather than ethnic groupings.

It must be remembered that the colonial legacy did little to instill Western concepts of libertarian press freedom in most African countries. It is worth noting the analysis of Russell Warren Howe, a foreign correspondent in Africa for many years: "The political and psychological attitude to the press is often determined by the absence or presence of a press tradition."[53] Thus, it is generally believed that Francophone Africa has a much more authoritarian view of the press than Anglophone Africa, where colonial officials allowed a degree of autonomy.

Social historian C. W. Black singles out black Africa for comment. Although parts of Asia also were under colonial rule, he contends that the traditional institutions were sufficiently developed to withstand the continuation of colonial patterns after independence. Africa, in contrast, had few cohesive institutions and was virtually forced to continue colonial models if the independent states were to meet and adapt to the challenge of modernity.[54]

It should be noted, however, that some anthropologists consider Black's interpretation somewhat simplistic and inaccurate. In their view, traditional African institutions were once present but generations of colonial rule and cultural imperialism destroyed parts of the African identity.

Regardless of these arguments, the nature of the contemporary press in black Africa has met with a degree of sympathy from journalists and scholars familiar with the continent. One common theme is the unfairness of comparing developing nations with press institutions in the developed countries of the West.

James M. Coltart, managing director of the Thomson organization told the Royal African Society in London in 1963, "It has taken many hundreds of years for us to get to this place and we cannot expect other people to accept it overnight."[55]

Another Britisher, William Francis, stated:

> Manifestly freedom of colonial rule is too young, the problems of establishing new nations too great, the consciousness

of internal challenge to national unity too strong and the economic basis for an independent press still too remote for the
principle of press freedom developed over the centuries in
the West to be as yet easily assimilated in these new nations
of . . . Africa. [56]

However, the argument is often advanced, that press controls in
Africa today are much harsher than controls during the early years of,
for example, the United States. In addition, it is said, the press models
are now developed and the African nations have no real excuse for
claiming underdevelopment. Just as they can easily adopt modern manu-
facturing processes, it is not really necessary for them to spend a long
period of time developing free press institutions.
Wilbur Schramm, however, is not so sure that the early years of
press development in the United States have relevance for Africa·

Indeed, it is probably wrong for us to expect a country
which is trying to gather together its resources and mobilize
its population for a great transitional effort to permit the same
kind of free, competitive, and sometimes confusing communication which we have become accustomed in this country.
This is a luxury which we can now afford. We could afford it
during our own period of economic development because we
moved slowly and had the resources of a wonderfully rich
continent behind us. A comparatively poor country, trying
to do in a few years what we did in a century, feels that it
can hardly afford such a luxury. It can hardly afford to have
its energies divided in any way. We must be prepared to sym-
pathize with this point of view, and to expect that as these
countries grow toward economic strength and political stability,
they will be more likely to encourage communication freedom. [57]

Although press freedom is generally seen as a luxury and not
entirely possible at present, it is interesting that many African journalists see this as only a temporary situation. Mathias Gbadoe, former
editor of Togo Presse, said:

We are not going to tolerate a press which becomes for
all eternity a mouthpiece of government or a political party
. . . . There is no doubt that freedom of speech becomes a
reality as soon as circumstances permit it. [58]

Black Africans studying in the United States also indicate that
contemporary restrictive press-government relationships are a temporary
situation. Some of the 33 students from 16 African countries enrolled
at Southern Illinois University indicated this in 1970 in a modified

Q-study. [59] Each subject was asked to rank 47 statements about the role of the press in Africa on a seven-point agree-disagree scale. The result was a six-factor solution.

The largest factor (type 1) consisting of eight students, indicated that mass communications should be a watchdog of government but control of the press in Africa is a "necessary temporary measure." Type 2 (five students) endorsed the idea of the press as neither a watchdog on government nor an agent of government. Type 3 (four students) felt that the press should be controlled by the government and should support policies of national leaders; these students were from Ethiopia, Somalia, and the United Arab Republic.

Type 4 (five students) seemed to be somewhat confounded. They tended to justify government control of the press but also endorsed a relatively free press. The students on this factor were from Zambia, Ethiopia, Tanzania, Nigeria, and Mali. Type 5 (seven students) did not feel strongly about any particular philosophy of the press but seemed to want a free press with somewhat contradictory controls.

On the sixth and final type (four students), it was felt that government held an exalted position and the press should support it. The students—from Malawi, Uganda, Upper Volta, and Tanzania—also felt that the press was relatively unimportant, with support of government policy its major duty.

The author of this study, F. L. Masha, apparently concluded that the last factor (Type 6) suggested another "theory of the press" in which a subservient press operated in a system where its posititon as a social institution was not yet recognized. In summary, the factor loadings generally showed that African students saw the press first as a political instrument and only second as an instrument of national development.

NOTES

1. Olav Stokke, "Mass Communication in Africa—Freedoms and Functions," in Reporting Africa, ed. Olav Stokke (Uppsala: Scandinavian Institute of African Affairs, 1971), p. 73.

2. Robert L. Nwankwo, "Utopia and Reality in the African Mass Media: A Case Study," paper presented at the African Studies Association Convention, Philadelphia, 1972, p. 1.

3. O. S. Coker, "Mass Media in Nigeria," in Mass Media Systems, ed. Royald D. Colle for the Department of Communication Arts, New York State Colleges of Agriculture (Ithaca, N. Y.: Cornell University, 1968), p. 42.

4. John C. Merrill, Carter R. Bryna, and Marvin Alisky, The Foreign Press (Baton Rouge: Louisiana State University Press, 1970), p. 288.

5. Area Handbook for Zambia, prepared by the Foreign Area Studies Program of the American Univeristy (Washington, D. C: U. S. Government Printing Office, 1969), p. 246.

6. K. W. Eapen, "Zana, An African New Agency," Gazette 18, no. 4 (1972): 205.

7. Ferdinand E. Mwanza, first secretary of the Embassy of Zambia, Washington, D. C., personal interview at the embassy on January 9, 1974. When asked to explain the definition of "objectivity" in the Zambian context, Mwanza said it was merely "by simple reason." He indicated that it was defined by the party so there was little question about what was "objective and truthful."

8. Herbert Passin, "Writer and Journalist in the Transitional Society," in Communication and Political Development, ed. Lucian W. Pye (Princeton, N. J.: Princeton University Press, 1963), pp. 122-23.

9. Richard Hall, "The Press in Black Africa; How Free Is It?" Optima 18 (March 1968): 66.

10. E. Floyd Sommerlad, "Problems in Developing a Free Enterprise Press in East Africa," Gazette 15, no. 2 (1968): 77.

11. Hilary B. Ng'weno, "The Nature of the Threat to Press Freedom in East Africa," Africa Today 16 (June, July 1969): 4.

12. John M. Ostheimer, Nigerian Politics (New York: Harper and Row, 1973), p. 96.

13. Colin Legum, chief ed., Africa Contemporary Record-Annual Survey and Documents 1972-73 (New York: Africana, 1973), p. C179.

14. Hall, "The Press in Black Africa," p. 17.

15. Titus Mukupo, "What Role for the Government in the Development of an African Press?" Africa Report 11 (January 1966): 39.

16. Charles Cutter, "Political Communication in a Pre-Literate Society: The Radio in Mali," paper presented to the annual meeting of the African Studies Association in Denver, November 3, 1971, p. 2.

17. John C. Condon, "Some Guidelines for Mass Communications Research in East Africa," Gazette 14, no. 2 (1968): 148.

18. John Condon, "Nation Building and Image Building in the Tanzania Press," The Journal of Modern African Studies 5, no. 3 (1967): 352.

19. Mathias Gbadoe, "Immediate Freedom of the Press in the Emergent Nations: Yes or No?" The Journalists' World 3, no. 1 (1965):5.

20. Fouroumo Kourouma, counselor of the embassy of Guinea, Washington, D. C., personal interview at the embassy on January 4, 1974.

21. Stokke, "Mass Communication in Africa," p. 86.

22. The Spark, Accra (Ghana), October 1, 1965. As cited in Don Dodson and William Hachten, "Communication and Development: African and Afro-American Parallels," Journalism Monographs, no. 28, (1973): 30.

23. Stokke, "Mass Communication in Africa," p. 109.

24. Christopher S. Clapham, Haile Selassie's Government (New York: Praeger Publishers, 1970), p. 187.

25. "A Decade After Independence, Two Africas Meet," IPI Report, April 1971, p. 3.

26. Sommerlad, "Problems in Developing a Free Enterprise Press in East Africa," p. 76.

27. Eddie Agyemang, "Freedom of Expression in a Government Newspaper in Ghana," in Reporting Africa, ed. Stokke, p. 50.

28. Theodore Magloe, "The African Press: Its Role," The Journalists' World 3, no. 4 (1966): 25.

29. Legum, Chief ed., Africa Contemporary Record—Annual Survey and Documents 1972-73, p. C182.

30. "President Kenyatta Airs Ownership Question," IPI Report, July-August 1968, p. 3.

31. M. J. Kenyatta, "An Address to the International Press Institute Conference in Nairobi, 1968," Africa Today 16 (June-July 1969):6.

32. A. A. Ojera, "Opening Remarks at Symposium on the Press in Africa," in Mass Thoughts, eds. Edward Moyo and Susan Rayner (Kampala: Makerere University Press, 1972), p. 155.

33. The African Journalist, December 1973, p. 4 (published by the International Press Institute, Zurich).

34. Area Handbook for the Democratic Republic of Sudan, prepared by the Foreign Area Studies Program of the American Univeristy (Washington, D. C: U. S. Government Printing Office, 1973), p. 214.

35. Derek Davies, "The State of the Press," Far Eastern Economic Review, Octover 9, 1971, 1. 21.

36. Ali A. Mazrui, "The Press, Intellectuals and the Printed Word," in Mass Thoughts, eds. Moyo and Rayner, p. 160.

37. Kenyatta, "An Address to the International Press Institute Conference in Nairobi 1968," p. 5.

38. "Role for Unity—If Press Has Freedom to Play It," IPI Report, July-August 1968, p. 10.

39. Ali A. Mazrui, Cultural Engineering and Nation-Building in East Africa (Evanston, Ill.: Northwestern University Press, 1972), p. 56.

40. Ibid., p. 56.

41. Ibid., p. 57.

42. Mazrui, "The Press, Intellectuals and the Printed Word," p. 164.

43. E. J. B. Rose, "Problems of the Press in Africa," report by the Institute of Mass Communications at Munster University, 1962, p. 63.

44. D. Nelson, "Government and the Free Press," in Mass Thoughts, eds. Moyo and Rayner, p. 168.

45. Kelvin G. Mlenga, "What Sort of Press Freedom?" The Journalists' World 3, no. 2 (1965): 15.

46. New York Times, October 28, 1973, p. 6.

47. Ely J. Kahn, The First Decade: A Report on Independent Black Africa (New York: W. W. Norton, 1972), p. 35.

48. Clair St. Drake, "Traditional Authority and Social Action in Former British West Africa," in Independent Black Africa: The Politics of Freedom, ed. William J. Hanna (Chicago: Rand McNally, 1964), p. 309. Readers interested in traditional communicatioñ systems for Africa should see Leonard Doob, Communication in Africa (New Haven: Yale University Press, 1961).

49. Area Handbook for Ethiopia, prepared by the Foreign Area Studies Program of the American University (Washington, D. C.: U. S. Government Printing Office, 1971), p. 322.

50. Daryl J. Hobbs, "Patterns of Communication in Malawi," paper prepared for the University of Missouri AID team charged with setting up a radio station in Malawi, 1966.

51. Magloe, "The African Press: Its Role," p. 23.

52. Guy M. Roppa, "Communication for Modernization in a Nomadic Society: Conditions and Prospects for Somalia," master's thesis, Indiana University, 1970, p. 221.

53. Russell Warren Howe, "Reporting from Africa: A Correspondent's View," Journalism Quarterly, 43 (Summer 1966): 316.

54. C. E. Black, The Dynamics of Modernization (New York: Harper Torchbooks, 1966), p. 124.

55. James M. Coltart, "The Influence of Newspapers and Television in Africa," African Affairs 62 (July 1963): 210.

56. Francis Williams, The Right to Know: The Rise of the World's Press (London: Longmans, 1969), p. 248.

57. Wilbur Schramm, "Communication Development and the Development Process," in Communications and Political Development, ed. Lucian W. Pye (Princeton, N. J.: Princeton University Press, 1963), p. 55.

58. Gbadoe, "Immediate Freedom of the Press in the Emergent Nations," p. 5.

59. F. L. Masha, "Attitudes of African Students Towards the Relationship Between the Government and the Press in Africa," master's thesis, Southern Illinois University, 1970.

3

OWNERSHIP AND CONTROL
FROM THE SAHARA TO
THE KALAHARI

Fewer daily newspapers are published in independent black Africa than any other region in the world. In an area twice the size of the continental United States, with a population of 240 million people, only 71 newspapers were being published in April 1974. [1]

More important, from the standpoint of controlling the flow of information, 47 of these newspapers, or two-thirds, are operated and owned directly by government or government-organized corporations. Another four dailies, 6 percent of the total, are owned and operated by ruling political groups in one-party states. The remaining 20 dailies (28 percent of the total) are privately owned.

Table 3.1 summarizes the number and ownership of dailies by country. It can readily be seen that over 70 percent of the 34 nations in black Africa only have daily newspapers owned by government or the ruling party. This percentage is bound to increase in the next four years since three of the privately owned dailies are already under direct government control or have announced plans to suspend publication.

In Cameroon, for example, La Presse du Cameroun, privately owned by French interests, will cease publication after the government launches two new dailies, one in English and the other in French. They are titled the Cameroon Tribune and La Tribune Camerounaise. [2] Essentially, they are the same newspaper in different languages.

The Daily Times of Malawi, at the present time, is privately owned in name only; it is reported that President H. Kamuzu Banda owns the majority of shares. [3] In Zambia, some observers say Lonrho, a British mining conglomerate with interests in at least eight African countries, no longer owns the majority of shares in the Times of Zambia. The newspaper, according to one report, was included when the Zambian government "purchased" 51 percent of Lonrho's copper interests in the country. [4] Although the exact ownership cannot be confirmed, it is known that President Kenneth Kaunda now appoints the editors on the Times of Zambia. [5]

TABLE 3. 1

Number and Ownership of Daily Newspapers

Nation	Number of Dailies	Category of Ownership		
		Government Ownership	Ruling Party	Private Interests
Botswana	1	1		
Burundi	1	1		
Cameroon	2	1		1
Central African Republic	1	1		
Chad	1	1		
Congo	1	1		
Dahomey	1	1		
Equatorial Guinea	0			
Ethiopia	6	5		1
Gabon	1	1		
Gambia	0			
Ghana	3	2		1
Guinea	1		1	
Ivory Coast	2	2		
Kenya	4			4
Lesotho	1	1		
Liberia	1	1		
Malawi	1			1
Mali	1	1		
Mauritania	1	1		
Niger	1	1		
Nigeria	14	7		7
Rwanda	0			
Senegal	1	1		
Sierra Leone	3	3		
Somalia	2	2		
Sudan	3		3	
Swaziland	0			
Tanzania	3	2		1
Togo	1	1		
Uganda	4	2		2
Upper Volta	3	2		1
Zaïre	4	4		
Zambia	2	1		1
Total	71	47	4	20

Most remaining dailies owned by private, commercial interests are found in two Anglophone nations, Nigeria and Kenya. Nigeria, the most populous country in black Africa, has at least seven dailies in private ownership ranging from the almost bankrupt West African Pilot to the wealthy and influential Daily Times group, which publishes nine general circulation publications and a number of trade journals.

As the largest publishing and printing service in black Africa, the group's flagship publication, the Daily Times, has the greatest circulation of any daily in Nigeria. Its sister newspaper, the Sunday Times, has an even higher circulation and claims to have the highest circulation and readership of any English-language weekly in Africa. Despite the trend for various Nigerian state governments to begin their own newspapers, the combined circulation of the Daily Times (200, 000) and the Sunday Times (350, 000) still exceeds the combined circulations of all daily and weekly government newspapers. [6]

Unlike the Nigerian commercial dailies, which face competition from an equal number of federal-and state-owned daily newspapers, the four dailies of Kenya are all privately owned. This makes Kenya the only nation in independent black Africa with a daily press completely in private hands. The nation's situation is even more unique in that these dailies are owned by foreign interests.

Privately owned dailies also are found in Ethiopia, Ghana, Tanzania, Uganda, and Upper Volta, but they are the exception instead of the rule.

In Ethiopia, the Italian-language daily Il Quotidiano Eritera remains in private ownership although it is closely supervised by the government. The newspaper is an anomaly since the country's five other dailies are government-owned. One explanation for the newspaper's status is the fact that it is published in Asmara, in Eritera. This area did not become a province of Ethiopia until 1962 and its predominant Muslim population has always had some autonomy over its local institutions. The future of Il Quotidiano Eritera, to a large extent, depends upon the final outcome of the Eritrean conflict with the government in Addis Ababa.

The Pioneer presently is the only privately owned daily newspaper in Ghana. It is published in Kumasi and must compete with the two government-owned capital dailies, the Daily Graphic and the Ghanian Times. The military regime of Colonel Ignatius Acheamong banned the newspaper in July 1972, but the ban was lifted in September of the same year.

Tanzania has embarked on an ambitious program of African socialism but one privately owned daily, Ngurumo, still exists in Dar es Salaam. It is a four-page tabloid published in Swahili by a group of local businessmen. By publishing in the lingua franca, it competes with the government-operated Daily News and TANU's party organ, Uhuru.

The future of privately owned dailies in Uganda will depend on the whip of General Idi Amin and how well these dailies adhere to the government line. Munno, the Roman Catholic daily published in the Luganda language, suspended publication in July 1972 for financial reasons but began publishing again later in the year. A second daily, Taifa Empya, also is published in the Luganda language.

L'Observateur of Ouagadougou, Upper Volta, is one of black Africa's newest independent dailies. It is owned by several local businessmen, and according to one report, "It is becoming the most widely read newspaper in the country."[7] As is the case for most privately owned dailies in Africa, its continued existence will depend on its ability to generate subscriptions and commercial advertising in a highly illiterate and poor country.

POLITICAL PARTY OWNERSHIP

The predominant pattern of daily newspaper ownership in independent black Africa is governmental, but a variation on the theme is the existence of national dailies owned and operated by the ruling political party.

However, this distinction becomes somewhat blurred in nations dominated by a single, institutionalized political party. One can legitimately argue that the ruling party in such nations is the ultimate source of all political power and the government is merely a vehicle for implementing programs established by party congresses.

In countries like Senegal and Ivory Coast, party officials also are government officials and it is difficult to separate functions. Laurent Fologo, editor of Fraternité-Matin, for example, is a member of President Houghouët-Boigny's cabinet as well as the ruling political bureau of the Parti Démocratique de Côte d'Ivoire. This makes it virtually impossible to determine whether the newspaper is controlled by the government or party.

One approach to resolving such ambiguity is to determine how the people of a nation perceive and conceptualize the ownership and control of their daily newspapers. The Sudan offers a good example. The nation's three dailies are operated by government-organized corporations but there is little doubt that the Sudanese Socialist Union exercises complete policy control. According to Omer El Hag Musa, minister of culture and information, "The Socialist Union is in full control of the press."[8]

In Guinea, Horoya has always been the official organ of the Parti Démocratique de Guinée (PDG). The country is a one-party state and President Sekou Touré is also secretary-general of the party. In 1968, he was reelected to another five-year term with 99.7 percent of the vote. President Touré's authority stems from his party office and it is generally recognized that the party possesses sovereign and exclusive control over all sections of national life. The party also operates and owns all media facilities.

Other daily newspapers in one-party states may also be under the direct control of the ruling political party, but only the Sudan and Guinea make a special point of enunciating the party's influence and control.

GOVERNMENT CORPORATIONS

A great majority of government-owned daily newspapers in independent black Africa are directly under the ministry of information or a similar government agency.

A few countries, however, have government-organized corporations in the hope that the daily newspapers can be financially self-supporting. These nations include the Sudan, Liberia, Ghana, and Tanzania.

The Sudan has the unique concept of two rival publishing houses although each operates under policy guidelines of the Sudanese Socialist Union. Each corporation publishes a major Arabic language daily newspaper. Al Sahafa, generally catering to rural interests, is published by Al-Ayam Publishing House; El Rai El Amm, published by a corporation of the same name, offers more foreign and urban news.

The existence of two rival publishing houses, according to Sudanese diplomat Hassan A. El Tayeb, is "a sort of competition for the better."[9] This element of competition is considered a substitue for the number of independently owned newspapers before the 1969 military coup. General Jaafar al Nimeiry and the Revolution Command Council nationalized the entire Sudanese press in August 1970 when it set up the two government publishing houses. In 1971, Nimeiry was elected president and the Sudanese Socialist Union was declared the only legitimate political party.

Each publishing house has a board of directors composed of governmental officials, party officials, and Sudanese intellectuals. Members, appointed by President Nimeiry, are all active members of the Sudanese Socialist Union. The official party viewpoint is implemented through the board of directors.

Liberia's only daily newspaper, the Liberian Star, also is organized under a government corporation although various government officials attempt to label it a newspaper owned by "leading Liberian citizens." However, all these citizens have positions in government and one informant states that the paper's directors are appointed by the government.[10] According to an employee of the Ministry of Information, "Government subsidizes all newspapers and therefore virtually controls all. The minister of foreign affairs is a brother of the managing editor of the only daily-Liberian Star."[11]

In Ghana, the Daily Graphic and the Ghanaian Times have been operated for a number of years by government corporations. The government appoints the directors, who primarily oversee the commercial interests of the corporations. The Daily News in Tanzania, known as the Standard before being nationalized in 1972, also is operated by a government corporation. The board of directors is directly appointed by President Julius Nyerere and includes government officials, leaders of the NANU party, and private citizens. [12]

NATIONS WITHOUT DAILY NEWSPAPERS

Four nations in independent black Africa have no daily newspapers or news bulletins. They all are small countries with limited populations: Equatorial Guinea, Gambia, Rwanda, and Swaziland.

Equatorial Guinea is the least populous country in black Africa, with only 300,000 people occupying a land area slightly larger than the state of Maryland. El Diario, once a daily newspaper in Spanish, became a semiweekly in December 1973. Renamed La Unidad, it publishes on Wednesdays and Saturdays with a press run of about 2,000. The printing facilities are modest; in early 1974 the newspaper received some new and reconditioned Chinese typesetting and printing equipment. La Libertad, another newspaper, is published irregularly. The Boletin Official is published even more sporadically. [13]

Gambia, sandwiched between Senegal and Guinea on a narrow strip of land, is the smallest nation in independent black Africa. The country's 300,000 people primarily rely on the government-operated Gambia News Bulletin for information. It is published three times a week and prints the same news that is read on Radio Gambia. In addition, there are government announcements, a lost-and-found column, and messages of public interest. Several private weeklies circulate in Gambia, including the Gambia Echo and Gambia Onward; their circulations are generally about 1,000 copies.

Rwanda, also about the size of Maryland, receives its daily information from radio broadcasts. [14] The only newspapers in the country, with a population of 3.6 million, are three weeklies. The main newspaper, Rwanda Carrefour d'Afrique, is operated by the Ministry of Information and is the major organ of government policy. This newspaper has a 9-by-12-inch format with 16 pages, usually run off on a mimeograph machine. There are editions in French, Kiswahili, and English.

A second weekly, Imvaho, is printed by the Rwanda government in the Kinyarwanda language. Kinamateka, published by the Roman Catholic Church, covers secular as well as church news.

Tiny Swaziland, an enclave of South Africa, primarily relies on South African newspapers for daily news. The Times of Swaziland, a weekly, is owned by the Argus group of South Africa.

It might be added that Botswana and Lesotho, although they have daily news bulletins, also rely on South African daily newspapers. The Daily News of Botswana is only a mimeographed bulletin so Johannesburg dailies enjoy a wide circulation in the country. Lesotho also has a daily mimeographed bulletin and generally relies on the Friend of Bloemfontein for daily news. The newspaper regularly carries an insert devoted to Lesotho news.

GOVERNMENT OWNERSHIP OF PRINTING PRESSES

For all practical purposes, the dominant trend in independent black Africa is toward goverment control and ownership of printing presses for newspapers and magazines. Almost half the governments already own more than 75 percent of printing presses in their nations (see Table 3.2). Such ownership, of course, tends to restrict and control nongovernmental access to mass media channels.

Ethiopia's monarchy probably had the longest history of exercising control over printing presses. Governmental ownership began more than 30 years ago when an imperial proclamation placed all printing presses under the jurisdiction of the Ministry of the Pen. Today, most major printing presses are owned by the government.[15]

Other governments with a high percentage of control over printing presses include Guinea, Ivory Coast, Sierra Leone, and Sudan. In Guinea, the nation's philosophy leaves no doubt about ownership of production facilities. Under Sekou Touré's scientific socialism, the government owns all industries and all workers are considered public employees. The Ivory Coast has only one major printing facility, owned by the government-operated Fraternité-Matin. Consequently, the printing plant publishes all sanctioned newspapers and magazines in the country.

Sierra Leone recently signed a contract with a foreign firm to upgrade the printing plant of the government-owned Daily Mail. Since the government already is the major publisher in the country, it is expected that this plant will solidify the government dominance in printing. In Somalia, the major printing plant is operated by the Ministry of Information. It was built in 1964 as a gift from the Soviet Union. According to one informant, "All printing presses are owned by the government."[16] This has occurred since October 1969, when the Somali government nationalized all private printing presses. The Sudan follows the same pattern; all publishing facilities there were nationalized in 1970.

Table 2.2 shows that only three nations—Cameroon, Kenya, and Zaïre—have less than 10 percent governmental ownership of major printing presses. In Kenya, the printing presses publish the country's four independent daily newspapers and do a variety of job printing; this balance helps keep the plants financially sound and not totally dependent on governmental contracts.

This is hardly the case in Zaïre, where daily and weekly newspapers are operated by the government. A number of privately owned printing plants publish these newspapers as a major source of income. According to one informant from Zaïre, "All major printing presses are commercial; but those which print government-supported newspapers are contractually dependent upon those papers [i.e., the government] for much of their income."[17]

The percentage of governmental ownership of printing presses is scheduled to significantly rise in Cameroon. The government is building the country's largest printing facility, which will publish the two new daily newspapers and a variety of other publications now handled in privately owned print shops. The percentage of governmental ownership also will benefit from the planned closing of La Presse du Cameroun, the nation's only independent daily.

THE DECLINE OF FOREIGN PRESS INTERESTS

The first decade after independence in black Africa took its toll of newspapers primarily owned by foreign interests. Independence brought nationalism into full bloom and many symbols of the colonial era, including foreign-owned newspapers, found their days numbered.

Most European-owned newspapers in Africa were either shut down or sold to the new governments after independence. The Daily Graphic of Ghana and the Daily Mail of Sierra Leone, owned by the London Daily Mirror group, were the first to become government-owned dailies. The de Breteuil family once had ambitions of establishing a group of newspapers in Francophone Africa, but independence saw the rapid demise of the plan. New governments in Guinea, Senegal, and Ivory Coast either purchased Breteuil newspapers outright or assumed majority control of the printing facilities.

Lord Thomson also had aspirations of establishing newspapers in black Africa, but by 1965 he had dissolved his ownership in Nigeria's Daily Express and Sunday Express. In the previous year, Thomson's Daily News in Rhodesia had been banned by the government. The last Thomson outpost was Malawi, where his Blantyre Printing and Publishing Company produced the Malawi Times. In January 1973, however, the newspaper and printing facilities were merged with the government-operated press. Thomson's newspaper was replaced by the new Daily Times, whose major stockholder is President Banda.

During the 1960s, the London Daily Mirror group (International Publishing Corporation) continued to operate the Daily Times in Lagos

TABLE 3. 2

Governmental Ownership of Printing Presses
for Newspapers and Magazines

	Number of Countries	Percentage of Total
Up to 10 Percent ownership:	3	8. 82
Cameroon, Kenya, Zaïre		
11 to 25 Percent ownership:	2	5. 88
Dahomey, Senegal		
26 to 50 Percent ownership:	5	14. 71
Lesotho, Liberia, Malawi,		
Uganda, Zambia		
51 to 75 Percent ownership:	8	23. 53
Burundi, Gambia, Ghana,		
Mali, Nigeria, Rwanda,		
Swaziland, Upper Volta		
Over 76 Percent ownership:	16	47. 06
Botswana, Central African		
Republic, Chad, Congo,		
Equatorial Guinea, Ethiopia,		
Gabon, Guinea, Ivory Coast,		
Mauritania, Niger, Sierra		
Leone, Somalia, Sudan,		
Tanzania, Togo		
Total	34	100

with Nigerian management, but the early 1970s found the foreign group
with a diminishing financial interest in black Africa's largest publishing
complex. The end of foreign investment was hastened in 1972 when
the government issued the Nigerian Enterprises Promotion Decree. It
required the Daily Times and other businesses to be exclusively owned
by Nigerians as of March 31, 1974. Consequently, the one million
shares owned by the Daily Mirror group were sold in early 1974 to the
Nigerian public. [18]

In East Africa, the takeover of foreign-owned newspapers was
more direct. The Standard of Tanzania, part of the European-owned
East African Standard group of Nairobi, was nationalized in 1972 and

merged with the government-owned Nationalist; the resulting newspaper
is the Daily News. Later in the same year, General Idi Amin of Uganda
nationalized the Uganda Argus, which had been owned by British and
Kenyan interests. One pretext for the takeover was a published article
about a sugar shortage in Uganda. The newspaper, now the Voice of
Uganda, is the government's official voice.
    Nationalization also has occurred in the Congo and Zaïre. The Congo
became Africa's first people's republic in 1969 and all foreign businesses
were nationalized. In Zaïre, the press was nationalized in 1972 and the
entire missionary press was terminated. According to one informant,
"All formerly European-owned newspapers were taken over by the government."[19]
    Other nations have not terminated foreign ownership but have
reduced it to minority financial interest. Fraternité-Matin in Ivory Coast,
for example, is 49 percent owned by the French Société Nationale des
Entreprises de Presse (SNEP). This group also owns France-Soir and
many other publications in France. Senegal has a similar agreement for
Le Soleil, which is 49 percent owned by French interests. Cameroon's
planned new governmental dailies have minority French ownership.
    In the 1970s, majority foreign ownership of newspapers and maga-
zines in independent black Africa is practically nonexistent. Kenya is
the only country where foreign-owned newspapers are firmly entrenched.
Lonrho now owns the East African Standard and the Swahili weekly,
Baraza. Majority interests in the Daily Nation and Taifa Leo are held
by the Aga Khan. In Swaziland, the Argus group of South Africa owns
and operates the weekly Times of Swaziland.
    Table 3.3 shows that 15 African nations now have definite policies
or governmental philosophies against majority foreign interest in print
media facilites. We have already mentioned the steps taken by many
nations on the list against foreign-owned media.
    The Marxist national ideology of Guinea, Congo, and Somalia
would automatically bar foreign ownership of newspapers. In nations
like Equatorial Guinea, one observer simply noted, "It is inconceivable
that foreigners could own newspapers."[20] Ethiopia has long had a
policy of press ownership, and foreign newspapers probably would not
be permitted. One Ethiopian wrote, "There is no law to this effect, but
there's certainly a policy."[21]
    Many of the 15 countries that do permit foreign ownership of news-
papers have attached qualifications. In Lesotho, for example, the
government asks for a percentage of the shares and profits. Rwanda
has no official policy regarding foreign ownership but, as one spokesman indicated, "The newspaper would have to respect the politics and
culture of the country."[22] Upper Volta also has no restrictions, but
representatives point out that any foreign investment would have to
meet government criteria on adhering to national goals and objectives.

TABLE 3. 3

National Policies Regarding Majority Foreign
Ownership of Media Facilities

	Number of Countries	Percentage of Total
Policies against foreign ownership: Congo, Equatorial Guinea, Ethiopia, Ghana, Guinea, Malawi, Mali, Mauritania, Nigeria, Sierra Leone, Somalia, Sudan, Tanzania, Uganda, Zaire	15	44. 12
Policies permitting foreign ownership: Botswana, Cameroon, Chad, Dahomey, Gabon, Gambia, Kenya, Lesotho, Liberia, Rwanda, Senegal, Swaziland, Togo, Upper Volta, Zambia	15	44. 12
Insufficient information: Burundi, Central African Republic, Ivory Coast, Niger	4	11. 76
Total	34	100

FOREIGN-OWNED BROADCASTING

Table 3. 3 primarily reflects governmental attitudes toward foreign ownership of print media. On broadcast facilities, most if not all of black Africa has a policy forbidding any foreign ownership of national radio and television services.

Specialized foreign-owned radio stations, however, do exist in at least four African countries. In three cases, the stations are operated by church groups and are primarily engaged in religious programming. Burundi, for example, has Radio Cordac, supported by the cooperative efforts of Protestant missionary organizations. ELWA, another religious station, broadcasts in 31 languages out of Liberia. Its programming is primarily religious but it also assists the government in generating support for plans of national development.

The Radio Voice of the Gospel, based in Ethiopia, is owned by the World Federation of Lutheran Churches and has an agreement with the government not to engage in partisan politics or impugn the beliefs and

practices of the Ethiopian Orthodox Church. The Radio Voice of the
Gospel, a shortwave station, can be heard throughout Africa.

International broadcasting is done from Liberia and Rwanda. The
Voice of America (VOA) maintains a transmitter in Liberia and the Voice
of Germany reaches most of Africa through a transmitter in Rwanda. The
French once operated Radio Brazzaville (Congo) as part of their international broadcasting, but in 1972 operations ceased. [23]

GOVERNMENT ENCOURAGEMENT OF PUBLICATIONS

Most governments in the world consider the flow of information a
vital part of national life. Consequently, a variety of policies are
implemented to encourage the circulation of newspapers and magazines.

In some countries, such as the United States, the encouragement
is indirect through reduced postal rates for printed matter. In many
Third World countries, however, the encouragement may be more direct,
in the form of governmental budgetary allocations.

The kind of governmental encouragement often determines the level
of control over a particular publication. A newspaper primarily dependent upon government subsidy and allocations, for example, often feels
pressure to support and endorse governmental policies. By the same
token, a newspaper receiving most of its revenue from subscriptions
and commercial advertising feels less pressure to strictly follow the
government's wishes.

The newspapers and magazines published in independent black
Africa rarely have the luxury of independent financial resources. In
such a setting, it has often been said that the press would not exist
in many countries, were it not for the government's financial support.
There is little consensus about the methods of government encouragement in most countries, but Table 3.4 offers a general idea of the
methods most prevalent currently in Africa. It can be seen that at least
70 percent of the countries use state subsidy and allocations.

This high percentage is not unusual given the fact that most daily
newspapers are operated by government in the first place. Although
privately owned newspapers rarely share in this form of governmental
encouragement, many do share the financial assistance of official
government advertising, which often makes the difference between profit and bankruptcy. At least 50 percent of the African nations encourage
the press with official government advertising, including legal notices,
proceedings of elective bodies, government employment opportunities,
and pleas for support of development plans.

Other forms of governmental encouragement include reduced postal
rates for periodicals, loans for printing equipment, and guaranteed
purchase of copies. More than a third of the African nations utilize

TABLE 3.4

Governmental Encouragement of Publications

Nation	Government Advertising	Loans for Equipment	Purchase of Copies	Reduced Postal Rates	Direct Budget Subsidy	No Special Action
Botswana					x	
Burundi	x			x	x	
Cameroon	x	x		x	x	
Central African Republic						x
Chad					x	
Congo					x	
Dahomey	x				x	
Equatorial Guinea						x
Ethiopia	x				x	
Gabon					x	
Gambia				x		
Ghana	x	x		x	x	
Guinea					x	
Ivory Coast	x		x		x	
Kenya	x	x		x		
Lesotho						x
Liberia	x	x			x	
Malawi	x				x	
Mali	x				x	
Mauritania					x	
Niger					x	
Nigeria	x			x	x	
Rwanda	x					
Senegal	x	x	x		x	
Sierra Leone		x			x	
Somalia					x	
Sudan	x			x		
Swaziland						x
Tanzania	x			x	x	
Togo			x		x	
Uganda	x			x		
Upper Volta				x	x	
Zaïre					x	
Zambia	x			x		
Total	17	6	3	12	24	4
Percentage	50	17.6	9.0	35.3	70.6	11.8

the concept of reduced postal rates but some do not extend the privilege to nongovernmental publications; Tanzania is a good example.

Loans for printing equipment are less known in black Africa and most governments claim this is not part of official policy. The Kenyan government can make loans to periodicals owned by private citizens, but this is rarely done. In Ghana, one informant says loans "happen in a blue moon."[24] Information from Gambia indicates that such a loan was once made to a periodical but this is not declared government policy.

Guaranteed purchase of bulk copies is even rarer in Africa. Less than 10 percent of the nations permit this, mainly because the direct governmental allocations often include free distribution of copies. Such is the case in Botswana. In the Ivory Coast, Fraternité-Matin is distributed free to all hotels and upper-echelon public employees. In Togo, each government ministry orders and pays for a number of subscriptions. This, in effect, spreads the cost of operating the nation's daily newspaper among a number of government departments.

Other government policies to encourage periodicals include reduced taxes on imported newsprint. Nigeria has no import duties on newsprint and Ethiopia has extremely favorable customs treatment for imported newsprint. In Cameroon, newspaper sales are exempt from the monthly turnover tax charged most businesses.

GOVERNMENT ALLOCATION OF NEWSPRINT

Most Third World countries, due to foreign exchange considerations, have policies regulating the amount of imported newsprint. The outflow of hard currency for foreign goods is a serious problem in terms of balance of payments, but the other edge of the sword can be the deliberate attempt to withhold newsprint from dissident publications.

Accordingly, it is important to look at the allocation of newsprint as a possible government control on the nongovernmental press. Do government publications, for example, have priority over those in the private sector?

Table 3.5 shows that about half the nations in black Africa generally allocate newsprint on the basis of need rather than type of ownership. In some countries, like Ghana, allocation of newsprint is proportional to circulation. Neighboring Nigeria has no fair-share allocation system; all newsprint purchases are done on competitive bidding and any newspaper can buy as much as it can afford.

Kenya has a predominantly privately owned press and one informant wrote, "We are allowed to import newsprint from overseas."[25] The nation, however, does have an exchange control commission and it is necessary to obtain authorization to buy newsprint abroad. Most publishers consider this a formality and, according to reports, no attempt

TABLE 3.5

Newsprint Allocation Priorities

	Number of Countries	Percentage of Total
Governmental and private periodicals equally treated: Cameroon, Dahomey, Gambia, Ghana,* Kenya, Lesotho, Liberia,* Malawi, Nigeria, Rwanda, Senegal, Swaziland, Tanzania,* Uganda,* Upper Volta, Zambia	16	47.06
Priority given to governmental publications: Burundi, Ethiopia*	2	5.88
Nongovernmental press does not exist: Botswana, Central African Republic, Congo, Equatorial Guinea, Gabon, Guinea, Ivory Coast, Mali, Mauritania, Niger, Sierra Leone, Somalia, Sudan, Togo, Zaïre	15	44.12
Insufficient information: Chad	1	2.94
Total	34	100

*Informants in these countries express a low level of consensus regarding governmental newsprint allocation policies.

has been made to use the exchange commission as a weapon to restrict the print media.[26]

Free access to imported newsprint is not so clear in other African countries. One Liberian informant wrote, "I believe each paper is free to acquire newsprint on the open market without government interference."[27] However, another wrote that the government controls virtually every newspaper except a few mimeographed magazines so allocation of newsprint is not a relevant problem. In Malawi, privately owned and governmental publications are equally treated but one observer noted, "It would be true [priority for government publications] if the demand outstripped the supply."[28]

Journalists in Tanzania also are divided on the question of government newsprint allocation policies. The press is predominantly state-owned but there are a few private newspapers, including the Swahili-language Ngurumo of Dar es Salaam. The process of receiving newsprint is probably the most frustrating part, however, since all requests must go through a subsidiary of the State Trading Corporation. According to one student of the Tanzanian press:

> The red tape involved in importing paper is wearisome and time consuming; after a pro-forma invoice is obtained from a supplier, an import license is issued; then follows a pre-shipment inspection at the paper factory abroad; a certificate of price of goods at market value is then issued, against which payment in foreign exchange can be made. [29]

Only two nations, Burundi and Ethiopia, actually have newsprint allocation policies favoring governmental publications. However, they also have a periodical press predominantly owned by the government.

Allocation of newsprint presents no problem in 44 percent of the African nations because there are no privately owned periodicals that require newsprint. It could be a problem in Botswana, but at the present time the only newspaper is the government-owned Daily News. Two independent fortnightlies have closed down for lack of funds and subscribers. Congo, Guinea, Sudan, Somalia, and Zaire have national ideologies that forbid private ownership of periodicals.

PREPUBLICATION REVIEW OF PERIODICALS

The most direct form of governmental press control is the prepublication review (censorship) of newspapers and magazines. Almost 60 percent of the nations in independent black Africa (see Table 3.6) exert this type of control. In most of the countries, it is a logical extension of a press totally owned and operated by the government. Such a situation makes prepublication review an inherent part of the press system.

The extent of systematized prepublication censorship, however, varies. The Daily News of Botswana, for example, pursues a relatively independent course despite its government ownership. One Botswana journalist explained, "The Daily News is not prior censored and acts relatively freely—basically because the government really is not very concerned about communications in the way one would perhaps expect." [30]

Ethiopia, on the other hand, had an elaborate prepublication review system under Emperor Haile Selassie. A censorship department within the Ministry of Information passed on all news stories before they were printed or broadcast. Its primary mission was to make sure all news jived with the country's foreign and domestic policies. Consequently, all copy passed through the censorship department before being distributed back to the department of press, radio, television, and the news agency. According to one report before the military take-over, "Dissemination policies are government formulated and even the

TABLE 3.6

Governmental Prepublication Review of Periodicals

	Number of Countries	Percentage of Total
Prepublication censorship: Botswana,* Cameroon, Central African Republic,* Congo,* Dahomey, Equatorial Guinea,* Ethiopia, Gabon,* Guinea,* Ivory Coast,* Malawi,* Mali,* Mauritania,* Niger,* Sierra Leone,* Somalia,* Sudan,* Togo, Upper Volta, Zaïre*	20	58.82
No prepublication censorship: Burundi, Chad, Gambia, Ghana, Kenya, Lesotho, Liberia, Nigeria, Rwanda, Senegal, Swaziland, Tanzania, Ugana, Zambia	14	41.18
Total	34	100

*Prepublication review is inherent in these nations since all periodicals are owned and operated by government.

privately owned media are subject to supervision by the Ministry of Information."[31]

The nature of censorship activities under the Emperor is illustrated by an Ethiopian editor. According to him, "There is censorship of those materials that are considered suggestive to investigating public disorder. We said nothing about Watergate, for example."[32]

Other nations have a formalized structure of prepublication review. The Central African Republic, for example, has an "editing and information control service" to examine all information before it is printed or broadcast. A censorship committee composed of party officials in Parti Congolais du Travail (PCT), the Congo's only political party, was organized in 1972. It succeeded previous censorship committees and all news reports must be circulated among the committee's members before being made public. Dahomey also has a censorship board which checks all copy prior to publication.

The Cameroon has a less formalized system of prepublication review. The government merely requires that the first copy of all privately owned newspapers must be given to the local district officer.

Several African nations had laws in the past requiring the government's approval of all news stories in advance of publication but these edicts have been revoked or fallen into disuse with the advent of a completely owned government press in these countries. This is the case in Mali, Mauritania, Niger and Togo which once required delivery of copy to government official from four to 24 hours prior to publication. Today, the editors are trusted government employees and such review is carried on within the newspaper office.

The remaining 14 countries in black Africa have no governmental prepublication review of newspapers and magazines, but many African journalists contend that indirect pressures are often effective substitutes. In Kenya, for example, informants agree that no prepublication review exists, but some are quick to add that government officials often talk to editors about the content and treatment of major news stories before publication.

Newspapers and magazines in Liberia also have no prepublication review but one informant said it is hardly needed because "The Star and The Age are 100 percent pro-government."[33] There is also a high level of self-censorship in Uganda in order to avoid a more formalized system of government censorship.

SUPPRESSION OF PUBLICATIONS

Another form of direct government press control is postpublication censorship. In many countries, governments ban, suspend, seize, or confiscate any newspaper or magazine when officials feel the content threatens public order and safety. The existence of such policies, without the benefit of judicial review to consider the validity of the threat, also leads to a degree of self-censorship by editors.

Independent black Africa is no exception to the concept that governments can and should prohibit published articles considered detrimental to national plans of development and tribal unity. Table 3.7 shows that 70 percent of the 34 nations have such policies.

The deliberate use of "policy" implies that individual governments often assume prohibitory powers although they are not provided in the constitution or in legislation. This is especially true in nations where a military regime has suspended the constitution and publications exist at the whim of officialdom. In other countries, there is no substantial body of written or case law to protect the press against arbitrary executive action.

One might argue that all governments have the ultimate authority to restrict the circulation of printed materials. This section, however, deals with governments that have announced such policies or have manifested them by suppressing publications for reasons other than libel, pornography, or specified sedition laws. In some countries, as noted in Table 3.7, informants express little consensus regarding the existence of official policies.

This is probably the result of fewer reported incidents where a government has taken steps to ban or confiscate an indigenous newspaper or publication. The advent of a wholly government-controlled press in Africa has made this form of control less necessary, but there have been some incidents in recent years. Ghana's last incident occurred in July 1972, when the military government banned the Pioneer and the Echo. The government has not exercised its banning power since that time, but some observers also note that the offending newspapers now have a more restrained editorial policy.

A newspaper started by a former civil servant was banned in Upper Volta during 1973. According to one source, the newspaper was banned because it contained only a long list of personal complaints against the government. [34] In Lesotho, Prime Minister Leabua Jonathan banned a cartoon strip several years ago because it depicted him in a "bad light."

The banning or confiscation of newspapers and magazines usually takes place after a military regime has taken power. It is a simple matter of executive decree without the benefit of legislation or constitutional provisions. In Uganda, General Idi Amin signed such a decree in early 1973, empowering his government to ban any newspaper for a specified or indefinite time. General Jurenal Habyalimane now rules Rwanda and it is understood that his government "can ban anything that would cause disorder or incite the people to revolt." [35]

Swaziland is not under a military regime but King Sobhuza II reclaimed his traditional power in April 1973 and suspended the nation's 1968 constitution. All political parties were banned and he announced that a royal commission would draft a new constitution. In the meantime, he has assumed all legislative, judicial, and executive powers. In such a setting, one Swazi journalist wrote, "Since April 1973 . . . there has been the machinery to close down newspapers any time. We have not been critical of the King but have given opinions [i.e., that preventive detention is bad]. There have been angry voices but no direct action." [36]

A fourth of the governments in independent black Africa do not have specific policies empowering them to ban, suspend, or seize newspapers in the interest of public order and safety. In most of these nations, however, voluntary self-restraint by editors appears to play a major role. According to one Botswana journalist, the government has no policy of banning but "there are limitations, not written but understood." [37]

In Kenya, the specter of self-restraint is always present. One journalist said there is no governmental policy to ban publications but "the government and press work under unwritten rules of self-restraint." [38] Another journalist states, "There's a lot of self-censorship for fear of government reprisals." [39] William Hachten once summarized the Kenya

TABLE 3. 7

Postpublication Censorship of Periodicals

	Number of Countries	Percentage of Total
Governmental policy exists:	24	70. 59
Burundi, Cameroon, Central African Republic, Chad, Congo, Dahomey, Equatorial Guinea, Ethiopia, Gabon, Ghana,* Guinea, Lesotho, Malawi, Mali, Senegal, Sierra Leone, Somalia, Sudan, Swaziland, Tanzania,* Togo, Uganda,* Upper Volta, Zaïre		
No governmental policy exists:	9	26. 47
Botswana, Gambia, Ivory Coast,* Kenya, Liberia, Mauritania, Nigeria,* Rwanda,* Zambia		
Insufficient information: Niger	1	2. 94
Total	34	100

*Informants in these countries express a low level of consensus concerning the government's official policy regarding banning, suspension, seizure, or confiscation of newspapers and magazines.

press by writing, "freedom of the press does not enjoy any substantial protection of the law; it exists at the whims of officialdom."[40] His point can readily be transferred to other nations in Africa.

AVAILABILITY OF OPPOSITION PARTY PUBLICATIONS

An opposition party press often provides citizens with a dissenting viewpoint regarding government plans and policies. At its best, it serves the valuable function of being a skeptic and watchdog of officials and programs. At its worst, a party press provides emotional polemics that offer few alternatives for solving the nation's problems.

The history of press development in other countries shows that an active party press often was the first step in the evolution of a diverse and relatively independent press system . The opposition press of Africa, however, seems to have come into existence only prior to independence when it rallied the people against continued colonial domination. Any number of nationalist movements used crudely printed newspapers to generate support for the ouster of colonial administrators.

Today, throughout independent black Africa, there are few news-papers and magazines owned and operated by opposition political parties. The advent of formal or de facto one-party states and military juntas has made such publications a virtually extinct species.

Table 3.8 shows that over 90 percent of the countries have no news-papers or magazines operated by opposition political parties. About 60 percent of this number are one-party states that, by definition, pro-hibit other political parties. At least 14 of the listed nations are formal one-party states in which only one party is legally and constitutionally recognized. Other nations, like Kenya, are de facto one-party states in that it is highly unlikely that additional political parties can become registered.

Most of the remaining nations with no political party opposition are under military regimes that have banned all political activity. Only in Lesotho and Swaziland have civilian governments taken steps to ban political parties and newspapers.

In Lesotho, Chief Jonathan banned all opposition party newspapers after his Basuto National Party (BNP) suffered a setback at the polls. Recent reports indicate that Lesotho may become a formal one-party state.[41] King Sobhuza II of Swaziland, as previously noted, banned all political publication in 1973.

Only Botswana, Gambia, and Liberia legally permit opposition parties to publish newspapers and magazines. However, the permission is a somewhat moot point since these three countries currently have no opposition newspapers. The one in Botswana went out of business for financial reasons, and the weeklies in Gambia consider themselves politically independent.

Opposition political party newspapers in Liberia are a possibility, but many observers consider their existence highly improbable. The True Whig Party has been in power for over 50 years and the opposition party is practically nonexistent in terms of organizational structure. In addition, a series of laws would effectively inhibit any opposition publication. Newspapers, under broadly interpreted guidelines, cannot print anything that would bring disrepute to the government. Unlike his predecessor, however, President William Tolbert is encouraging more public discussion of political issues.

Upper Volta, until recently, had at least three political parties and an equal number of party publications. These existed under the watchful eye of the military, which was guiding the nation back to complete civilian rule. In February 1974, however, the military banned all political activity to save the country from "squabbling politicians."[42] One journalist in Upper Volta wrote, "The publications of the political parties are now suspended and the political parties don't exist." He

TABLE 3. 8

Availability of Opposition Party Publications

	Number of Countries	Percentage of Total
Political parties and publications are presently banned: Burundi, Central African Republic, Dahomey, Ghana, Lesotho, Mali, Nigeria, Rwanda, Somalia, Swaziland, Uganda, Upper Volta	12	35.29
Formal or de facto one-party states with no opposition political parties: Cameroon, Chad, Congo, Equatorial Guinea, Ethiopia, [a] Gabon, Guinea, Ivory Coast, Kenya, Malawi, Mauritania, Niger, Senegal, [b] Sierra Leone, Sudan, Tanzania, Togo, Zaïre, Zambia	19	55.88
Publications of opposition parties legally permitted: Botswana, Gambia, Liberia	3	8.83
Total	34	100

[a] Ethiopia, then a traditional monarch with no party tradition, was included in this category only for comparative analysis.

[b] A new political party, the Senegalese Republican Party (PRS), was being formed in the fall of 1974.

expressed optimism about the future of the press in his country, however, because Lieutenant Colonel Bila Zagre, minister of information, was a "liberal."[43]

NOTES

1. The number of daily newspapers, a listing as of April 1974, is based on crosschecking a variety of primary and secondary sources. It should be noted that there is very little consensus among press directories. The number of daily newspapers ranges from 116 in the UNESCO Statistical Yearbook (1972) to 67 in Feuereisen and Schmache,

The Press in Africa (1973). Even respondents from the various nations with multiple dailies express little consensus. In Nigeria, for example, respondents to the mail questionnaire gave answers ranging from 9 to 23. In another case, the Zaïre embassy in Washington, D. C., claimed there were 14 dailies in the country. Crosschecking, however, confirmed the existence of only four dailies. This listing, then, is subject to constant revision and should only be used for general comparative purposes.

2. "Two New Dailies for Cameroon, " The African Journalist, March 1974, p. 7 (published by the International Press Institute, Zurich.

3. Comment on mail questionnaire from Malawi, anonymous.

4. Ferdinand E. Mwanza, first secretary of the embassy of Zambia, Washington, D. C., personal interview on January 9, 1974.

5. President Kaunda recently dismissed Dunstan Kamana as editor of the Times of Zambia and appointed the country's representative to the United Nations in his place.

6. Alhaji Babatunde Jose, "The Press in Nigeria, " speech at the opening session of the Distripress in Athens, Greece, on October 23, 1973.

7. Letter from Stanley Alpern, United States Information Service, Ouagadougou, Upper Volta, October 2, 1973.

8. Letter from Omer El Hag Musa, minister of culture and information, Khartoum, Sudan, February 2, 1974.

9. Hassan A. El Tayed, cultural counselor of the embassy of Sudan, Washington, D. C., personal interview on January 2, 1974.

10. Comment on mail questionnaire from Liberia, anonymous.

11. Comment on mail questionnaire from Liberia, anonymous.

12. Hamza Aziz, political affairs counselor at the embassy of Tanzania, Washington, D. C., personal interview on January 7, 1974.

13. Letter from U. S. diplomat who wishes to remain anonymous, January 29, 1974.

14. Ildephonse Munyeshyaka, first secretary of the embassy of Rwanda, Washington, D. C., personal interview on January 11, 1974.

15. Area Handbook for Ethiopia, prepared by the Foreign Area Studies Program of the American University (Washington, D. C.: U. S. Government Printing Office, 1971), p. 322.

16. Comment on mail questionnaire from Somali, anonymous.

17. Comment on mail questionnaire from Zaïre, signed.

18. Letter from Mrs. Funke Olaleye, secretary to Alhaji Babatunde Jose, chairman of the Daily Times, Lagos, Nigeria, March 19, 1974.

19. Comment on mail questionnaire from Zaïre, signed.

20. Letter from U. S. diplomat who wishes to remain anonymous, January 29, 1974.

21. Comment on mail questionnaire from Ethiopia, signed.

22. Interview with Munyeshyaka, January 11, 1974.

23. Letter from C. Massieu, Office de Radiodiffusion-Télévision Française, (ORTF), Paris, February 25, 1974.

24. Comment on mail questionnaire from Ghana, signed.

25. Comment on mail questionnaire from Kenya, signed.

26. Joseph Healey, "Press Freedom in Kenya," report prepared for the Freedom of Information Center at the University of Missouri at Columbia, December 1967, p. 4.

27. Comment on mail questionnaire from Liberia, signed.

28. Comment on mail questionnaire from Malawi, anonymous.

29. Michael Traber, "Kiongozi of Tanzania: Development for Self-Reliance," a press survey compled for the Department of Communications, Tanzania Episcopal Conference (Kitwe, Zambia, 1973), p. 32.

30. Comment on mail questionnaire from Botswana, signed.

31. Area Handbook for Ethiopia, p. 321.

32. Comment on mail questionnaire from Ethiopia, anonymous.

33. Comment on mail questionnaire from Liberia, signed.

34. Dominique B. Sisso, counselor at the embassy of Upper Volta, Washington, D. C., personal interview on January 11, 1974.

35. Interview with Munyeshyaka, January 11, 1974.

36. Comment on mail questionnaire from Swaziland, signed.

37. Comment on mail questionnaire from Botswana, anonymous.

38. Comment on mail questionnaire from Kenya, signed.

39. Ibid.

40. William A. Hachten, Muffled Drums (Ames: Iowa State University Press, 1971), p. 217.

41. Africa: South of the Sahara (London: Europa Publications, 1972), p. 423.

42. New York Times, February 10, 1974.

43. Letter from R. Sissao, Le Chef de Centre, Service de L'Information, Bobo-Dioulasso, Upper Volta, February 13, 1974.

4

ACCESS RESTRAINTS
AND LEGAL PROTECTION
OF JOURNALISTS IN
BLACK AFRICA

Government ownership of periodicals and printing facilities is one form of restricting citizen access to mass media channels. Another equally important press control is the licensing and certification of journalists.

Such a control, many governments claim, simply assures that working journalists are competent and qualified to handle the dissemination of information to millions of people. Advocates of the libertarian press concept, however, claim that licensing and certification procedures are tantamount to controlling access to the press. A working journalist, dependent upon government permission to earn a living, is less likely to serve as a public watchdog or uncover stories potentially embarrassing to government officials.

Certification or licensing in the context of press-government controls for proper identification. It means that some nations require individuals to meet specific qualifications in training or political ideology to be eligible for journalistic employment.

Table 4.1 shows that almost half of the black African nations require licensing or certification of journalists. Since eight of these nations have a wholly government-owned press, and all journalists there by definition are employees of government, the table attempts to indicate the nations that have certification requirements over and above those needed for government employment.

In the Sudan, for example, journalists must have formal journalism training, talent, and membership in the country's only political party, the Sudanese Socialist Union. The Sudanese Press Corporation, which directs operation of the country's print media, registers and certifies all journalists for employment. Certification of journalists, according to one report, is "dependent upon an ideological framework considered appropriate to the goals of national and social development."[1]

The government-owned press of Zaïre also requires formal journalism training. A prospective employee on a newspaper of magazine must attend the country's institute of journalism for a specific time. In Cameroon, working journalists must have a press card from the Ministry of Information. The card, however, is not issued until the applicant has two years of working experience as a journalist, usually as an apprentice. Only after a press card is issued can the individual begin to call himself a pressman and cover various governmental functions.

Ethiopia does not require an apprenticeship or formal training but does have a qualifying examination before a journalist can receive working papers. Most journalists work for government publications and the Ministry of Information usually assigns them to a particular newspaper or magazine after their "reliability and loyalty" have been certified. Individual editors, however, have the right to reject the Ministry of Information recommendation if they feel the person does not meet their specific needs.

An equal number of African nations, 15 in all, have no specific requirements for the licensing and certification of newsmen. Most of these nations have both governmental and nongovernmental newspapers and magazines. They generally require journalists to have a press card but reports indicate that few restrictions of a political nature are imposed. Other nations, like Kenya and Swaziland, require work permits for journalists, as for all other employed persons.

Although there is insufficient information to classify the Central African Republic, Niger, Ivory Coast and Malawi, the first three have a wholly government-owned press. Consequently, journalists are generally certified as loyal government employees.

REGISTRATION OF NONGOVERNMENTAL PRINT MEDIA

Nongovernmental newspapers and magazines subject to registration and licensing by the state have been used as an index of press control in several worldwide press freedom studies. Libertarians contend that any license to permit publication can be withdrawn if the periodical becomes too critical or skeptical of government policies and officials.

The concept of press control is inherent in any licensing or registration mechanism, but in Africa the criterion appears to lose much of its relevance. Black African informants and diplomatic representatives do not perceive registration of print media as an index of potential editorial control and restraint, but merely a requirement placed on all business enterprises. Registration in most African countries is not for suppression but for the purposes of establishing financial accountability and collecting taxes.

Table 4.2 shows that every African nation with elements of a nongovernmental press, with the exceptions of Liberia and Rwanda, has required registration and licensing. Most also license and register all

TABLE 4.1

Government Licensing of Journalists

	Number of Countries	Percentage of Total
Journalists licensed or certified by government: Burundi, Cameroon, Chad, Congo, Dahomey, Equatorial Guinea, Ethiopia, Gabon, Guinea, Lesotho, Mali, Somalia, Sudan, Uganda, Zaïre	15	44.12
No licensing or certification of journalists: Botswana,* Gambia,* Ghana, Kenya, Liberia, Mauritania, Nigeria, Rwanda, Senegal, Sierra Leone,* Swaziland, Tanzania, Togo, Upper Volta,* Zambia	15	44.12
Insufficient information: Central African Republic, Ivory Coast, Malawi, Niger	4	11.76
Total	34	100

*Informants in these countries express a low level of consensus regarding licensing and certification of journalists by government.

business enterprises so the criterion is ambiguous and not a good index of press restraint.

Licensing is not uncommon for newspapers, regardless of whether they are government-owned or independently owned. Nigeria, Ghana, and Tanzania are a few of the nations that have this policy. In Nigeria, all newspapers must be registered and a signed copy of every issue must be deposited with the government. The name and address of both the publisher and editor must appear in every issue.

Fourteen nations in Africa have a wholly government-owned press, so the criterion regarding nongovernmental publications does not apply to them. However, a check of these countries shows that two-thirds would license a nongovernmental publication if the opportunity presented itself.

Although periodicals conceivably could have their publishing licenses revoked by the government, most informants in Africa feel this is unlikely. In most cases, they say, the government has other powers at its command to close a publication for political reasons.

TABLE 4.2

Required Registration of Nongovernmental Print Media

	Number of Countries	Percentage of Total
Registration required: Botswana, Burundi, Cameroon, Chad, Dahomey, Ethiopia, Gambia, Ghana, Kenya, Lesotho, Malawi, Nigeria, Senegal, Swaziland, Tanzania, Uganda, Upper Volta, Zambia	18	52.94
Registration not required: Liberia, Rwanda	2	5.88
Nongovernmental press does not exist: Central African Republic, Congo, Equatorial Guinea, Gabon, Guinea, Ivory Coast, Mali, Mauritania, Niger, Sierra Leone, Somalia, Sudan, Togo, Zaïre	14	41.18
Total	34	100

Direct suppression is possible in most nations on the basis of ill-defined sedition laws, the public order and safety, or the national interest.

EXECUTIVE CONTROL OF THE JUDICIAL SYSTEM

Ralph L. Lowenstein found in his 1966 Press Independence Critical Ability (PICA) study that nations with a high degree of press freedom also have an independent judiciary. He later amplified this finding to state that a nation's press system is free, not necessarily because of constitutional guarantees but because an unintimidated judiciary protects the press against government encroachment. [2]

Consequently, it is important to find out if the judicial systems of independent Africa are free from manipulation and control by the executive and legislative branches of government. Two indexes are used.

The first deals with the appointment and dismissal of judges; it is not uncommon for the head of a country to appoint judges, but the critical point is whether the judges also can be removed by the executive at will. In other words, are there adequate safeguards to prevent the removal of judges who become politically unpopular with a current government?

The second criterion involves the judiciary's authority to determine the constitutionality of government laws and regulations. In many countries, this power is not bestowed upon the judicial system. If the right of review is not guaranteed, the judicial mechanism has little authority to dissuade governments wishing to suppress publications by legislation and executive orders, despite free press guarantees in the constitution.

Table 4.3 classifies the African nations according to the executive branch's power to appoint and dismiss judges without due process. It is based on what actually occurs in a country, not theoretical pronouncements. Seen in this context, an independent judiciary is a rarity in Africa, with more than 75 percent of the nations having no independent judiciary as understood in Western terms.

Of these 26 nations, at least nine are under military leadership, with civilian provisions for an independent judiciary either suspended or amended. Uganda and Mali, for example, have suspended the civilian legal system and instituted military courts. In Nigeria, a civilian judiciary still functions but its powers are limited in terms of reviewing the legality of government decrees.

Another 11 nations on the list are formal one-party states where the ruling political hierarchy exerts a great influence on judicial appointments and dismissals. In Mauritania, for example, the Parti du Peuple Mauritanien (PPM) appoints and approves judges for tenure on the basis of political loyalty. Guinea has a similar system; the central political bureau has complete power to appoint and dismiss judges. Two nations, Ethiopia and Swaziland, are monarchies with all branches of government controlled by imperial wishes.

Kenya presents a less clear concept of executive power to dismiss judges. Kenyan journalists agree that President Jomo Kenyatta has the power to dismiss judges, but others say this power is diluted because he must obtain cabinet approval. Since the nation is a one-party state for all practical purposes, Kenyatta does have a great deal of centralized power.

Only seven nations, or 20 percent of the total, have a judiciary somewhat insulated from control by the executive branch. The degree of insulation, however, is not accurately known. Ghana, for example, is presently under a military regime. Botswana, on the other hand, has a strong civilian government and all judges are given definite terms of office, except the chief justice, who is appointed for life.

A related index of potential press control is the ability of country's judiciary to review the constitutionality of any legislation or regulations that might infringe on freedom of the press as defined in the national

TABLE 4. 3

Executive Control of Judicial System

	Number of Countries	Percentage of Total
Judiciary subject to executive control: Burundi, Cameroon, Central African Republic, Chad, Congo, Equatorial Guinea, Ethiopia, Gabon, Gambia,* Guinea, Ivory Coast,* Kenya, Lesotho, Malawi, Mali, Mauritania, Nigeria, Rwanda, Somalia, Swaziland, Tanzania, Togo,* Uganda,* Upper Volta,* Zaïre, Zambia	26	76. 47
Judiciary insulated from executive control: Botswana, Dahomey,* Ghana, Niger,* Senegal, Sierra Leone,* Sudan	7	20. 59
Insufficient information: Liberia	1	2. 94
Total	34	100

*Informants in these countries express a low level of consensus regarding executive control of the judiciary.

constitution. Judicial review offers a buffer zone between press and government and often can check governmental abuses of press freedom.

Table 4. 4 shows that only nine nations in independent black Africa have the concept of judicial review. More than half of the 34 nations do not utilize their judicial systems in this way. Eight countries—Burundi, Dahomey, Ghana, Mali, Rwanda, Somalia, Togo, and Uganda—are military regimes and constitutions are suspended. In such cases, there is no basic document for judges to interpret.

The constitutions of Lesotho and Swaziland also are suspended at the present time, although the governments remain in civilian or royal control. Other nations with no judicial review are formal one-party states. In Guinea, for example, only the party hierarchy has the authority to interpret the constitution. Zaïre has a similar structure and all judicial decisions are made in the name of the president.

Three-fourths of the 18 nations with a lack of judicial review are similarly classified in a previous study published in 1970. [3] Central African Republic, Gabon, Upper Volta, and Zambia are among the

TABLE 4.4

Judicial Review of Legislation and Edicts

	Number of Countries	Percentage of Total
Judicial system reviews constitution-ality: Equatorial Guinea, Gambia, Kenya, Liberia, Mauritania, Nigeria, Sierra Leone, Sudan, Tanzania*	9	26.47
Judicial system lacks power to deter-mine constitutionality: Burundi, Chad, Congo, Dahomey, Ethiopia, Ghana, Guinea, Ivory Coast,* Lesotho, Malawi, Mali, Rwanda, Senegal,* Somalia, Swaziland, Togo, Uganda, Zaïre	18	52.94
Insufficient information: Botswana, Cameroon, Central African Republic, Gabon, Niger, Upper Volta, Zambia	7	20.59
Total	34	100

*Informants in these countries express a low level of consensus regarding the judiciary's power to review the constitutionality of legislation and edicts.

nations not classified in Table 4.4, but this 1970 study indicates a lack of judicial review in these countries, too.

Tables 4.3 and 4.4, taken together, show that the press in most black African countries cannot depend upon an independent judiciary to protect it from possible government control and takeover.

PREVENTIVE DETENTION ACTS

The lack of an independent judiciary to effectively review the con-stitutionality of government actions also permits the existence of pre-ventive detention acts. These laws enable a government to detain citizens without charge or trial.

Preventive detention policies create a chilling effect on the free flow of information because a government official becomes the sole

TABLE 4. 5

Existence of Preventive Detention Acts

	Number of Countries	Percentage of Total
Nations with preventive detention acts: Cameroon, Central African Republic, Chad, Dahomey, * Equatorial Guinea, * Kenya, Lesotho, * Malawi, Mali, Nigeria, Sierra Seone, Somalia, Sudan, * Swaziland, Tanzania, Togo, * Upper Volta, * Zaïre	18	52. 94
No preventive detention acts: Botswana, Ethiopia, Gabon, * Gambia, * Ghana, Guinea, Liberia, Mauritania, Niger, Rwanda, Senegal, Zambia	12	35. 29
Insufficient information: Burundi, Congo, Ivory Coast, Uganda	4	11. 77
Total	34	100

*Informants in these countries express a low level of consensus regarding the existence of preventive detention acts.

arbiter of which published stories are prejudicial to the national interest. For journalists wishing to stay out of jail, preventive detention acts are a government control on the press.

Table 4. 5 shows that over half the black African nations have preventive detention acts. In some cases, preventive detention is only used under emergency conditions, but these can last for years. Nigeria is a good example. That country has been under a state of emergency since the 1966 military coup and all citizens are subject to arrest without warrant and detention without trial.

One Nigerian journalist wrote, "The government takes every opportunity to declare its belief in press freedom but there have been many cases of arbitrary arrests and detention of journalists."[4] Alhaji Babatunde Jose, chairman of the Daily Times group, said, "almost every editor of any important newspaper, including those owned by the government, has seen the inside of a police cell or army orderly room."[5]

These editors include L. K. Jakande of the Nigerian Tribune, who also is the immediate past chairman of the International Press Institute. He was detained by the military for 16 days in 1969 for writing editorials advocating an return to civilian rule. Later in the same year, Ayo Adedun, editor of the government-owned Daily Sketch, was detained by military authorities. In more recent years, Chief Ola, news editor of the Daily Times (Lagos), was detained for a month after writing an article on the selection of a new principal for Ibadan Polytechnic.

Detentions in 1974 included Minere Amakiri, chief correspondent of the Nigerian Observer, who wrote a story about the pay demands of teachers in Three Rivers State. Royin Johnson, acting editor of the independent Nigerian Daily News, was detained by police for five hours after the newspaper criticized increases in bus fares.

One Nigerian observer noted that the state governments, administered by military governors appointed by the federal government, are the prime offenders in the detention of journalists. This is done primarily for harassment. The trend, however, seems to be for shorter periods of detention and less frequent arrests of journalists.[6] Self-censorship by editors, coupled with vigorous press protest when a journalist is arrested, are probably the causes.

In Malawi, however, preventive detention shows no evidence of easing. At least eight Malawian journalists have been detained without charge or trial since May 1973. President H. Kamuzu Banda ordered them detained for stories dealing with alleged troop clashes on the Mozambique border and has given no indication that they will be released soon. Thus, the specter of preventive detention has effectively curtailed the activities of all Malawian journalists.

Kenya has a preventive detention act dating back to 1966, the same year as the military coup in Nigeria. Under the act, the government has broad powers to detain citizens and censor newspapers. In recent years, however, there have been no reported incidents of a journalist being detained under the act.

In Swaziland, King Sobhuza II has issued a decree calling for the detention of citizens for up to 60 days without formal charges. According to informants in the country, the decree has been used against opposition political leaders but no journalists have yet been detained. Zaïre and Mali also have preventive detention, but no limitation of time is specified. According to a diplomat from Rwanda, the government can detain a citizen indefinitely "until all information regarding the case is gathered."[7]

Thirty-five percent of the African nations (see Table 4.5) have no preventive detention acts on the books. Botswana and Liberia, however, provide that detention can take place if the legislative branch declares a state of emergency. Ghana, despite its military government, does not utilize preventive detention, but one journalist was quick to add, "Some, including myself, have been militarily grilled for statements considered prejudicial to the national interest."[8]

Ethiopia does not have preventive detention of journalists, but one informant wrote, "The question does not arise because there is prepublication review of material."[9] Mauritania and Sudan also lack such policies simply because all journalists are employed by the government. It is highly unlikely that they would write or publish stories that would lead to preventive detention.

FINES AND IMPRISONMENT

A press control matter closely related to preventive detention is the government's power to fine or imprison journalists who officials feel have shown disrespect for the country's institutions and leadership. "Disrespect" is rather broadly interpreted in some countries as a threat to the nation's unity and harmony. This means that journalists can be punished on any number of broad grounds generally outside the usual grounds of libel, pornography, or even sedition. In black Africa, a survey shows that most fines and imprisonments are directed at journalists who have questioned or criticized government policies.

At least five nations provide examples in recent years. In Liberia, a reporter was fined and imprisoned for writing an article revealing information about foreign concessions in the country. He was accused of abusing the nation's press freedom and found it impossible to obtain employment as a journalist after his release from jail.[10] Revealing information also is a hazard in Uganda, where a local journalist who reported details of threats against foreign residents was accused of inciting potential violence.

Religious publications also may run afoul of government sensibilities. The editor of Leselinyana la Lesotho was jailed in 1972 by Prime Minister Leabua Jonathan for publishing stories about irregularities in government.[11] In neighboring Tanzania, the editor of Kiongozi was fined in 1970 after he printed articles criticizing the national service. The articles alleged that too many young girls were becoming pregnant while serving in Tanzania's version of the Peace Corps.[12] The imprisonment of journalists in Malawi already has been discussed in relation to preventive acts.

Although these cases are isolated examples, Table 4.6 shows that they could happen in 85 percent of the black African countries. Conditions for fine and imprisonment of journalists vary, but the effect is the same—indirect government control of news content.

Many nations, like Botswana, use an official secrets act that is broadly interpreted to include any information that the current government does not want released. In Liberia, it is considered sedition to show disrespect of the president because it can "bring disintegration into the organization of the government."[13] Other nations have spe-

TABLE 4.6

Imprisonment of Journalists for "Disrespect"
and Criticism of Government

	Number of Countries	Percentage of Total
Journalists can be fined or imprisoned for criticism of government: Botswana, Burundi, Cameroon, Central African Republic, Chad, Congo,* Dahomey, Equatorial Guinea, Ethiopia, Gabon, Gambia, Ghana, Guinea, Kenya, Lesotho, Liberia, Malawi, Mali, Mauritania, Niger, Nigeria, Rwanda,* Somalia, Sudan, Tanzania,* Togo, Uganda, Upper Volta, Zaïre	29	85.29
No fine or imprisonment for criticism of government: Swaziland, Zambia	2	5.88
Insufficient information: Ivory Coast, Senegal, Sierra Leone	3	8.83
Total	34	100

*Informants in these countries express a low level of consensus regarding the consequences of journalistic criticism.

cific press laws. A law dating back to 1968 in Chad makes it illegal to publish information that might jeopardize "the honor of institutions, the internal and external security of the state, public peace, the moral health of the people, or the edification of the Republic."[14]

Some nations have laws making it an offense to publish or reproduce false statements, rumors, or reports. In Ghana, the fine can be up to £235 and three years in prison. One Ghanaian journalist preferred to use the word "disciplined" instead of fine or imprisonment. He wrote, "In some instances, we are required to publish an apology, though one may be fined in severe cases."[15] Another Ghanaian journalist cited the effect of the law: "Most journalists apply voluntary censorship from bitter experience."[16]

Ethiopia also has a set of elaborate rules and regulations that can result in journalists being fined or imprisoned. Their foundation was the tradition that the person of the emperor was inviolable. For example, a news story that used the emperor's name could not precede his name

by that of another person, and all references to Haile Selassie were
capitalized. Journalists also risked punishment if they covered a broad
range of events. One American scholar of the press who conducted
field work in Ethiopia said:

> Coverage of dissident elements in Ethiopian society-
> student demonstrations, strikes, terrorist activities of the
> Eritrean Liberation Front, etc. — is absolutely and uncondi-
> tionally forbidden, as are items which depict poverty or
> disease in the country. [17]

Journalists in Kenya and Nigeria can be fined or imprisoned for a
variety of political reasons, but such measures are rarely used. Authorities in Nigeria prefer harassment to enforce conformity. Journalists
in Kenya also are intimidated and risk jail for "destructive criticism, "
which is defined as criticism that does not offer any constructive alternatives. [18] Another method in Kenya, where there are many expatriate
newsmen, is deportation.

One long-time journalist in Kenya agreed that fines and imprisonment were possible but added, "The press censors itself. Expatriates
owning newspapers and magazines would be deported quickly if they
stepped over the line. Criticism of government must be very limited.
No criticism of the president is permissible. "[19]

Journalists implying disrespect for government leaders and policies
are a rarity in Africa. Individuals could be fined or jailed in most of the
34 nations but, as one Cameroon informant wrote, "Journalists don't
do that here. "[20] A journalist in Ivory Coast said the structure of the
press (government-owned) makes fines or imprisonment unlikely. This
also is true in nations like Guinea, Mali, Mauritania, and Sudan.

REQUIRED POSTING OF BOND

The requirement that nongovernmental newspapers and magazines
post bonds in order to obtain permission to publish dates back to the
colonial era. British administrators in East and West Africa found
bonds a good way to discourage the proliferation of newssheets written
by aspiring nationalist editors.

A large bond not only discouraged many would-be editors but also
made the press more cautious since many editors could not afford to
lose their posted bonds. This method of government control is still
utilized in countries like South Vietnam. Table 4.7, however, shows
that required posting of bond has virtually disappeared in black Africa.
One reason is the advent of a wholly government-owned press in 14
nations.

TABLE 4.7

Required Posting of Bond for Nongovernmental Print Media

	Number of Countries	Percentage of Total
Bond required: Gambia,* Kenya	2	5.88
Bond not required: Botswana, Burundi, Cameroon, Chad, Dahomey, Ethiopia, Ghana, Lesotho,* Liberia, Malawi, Nigeria, Rwanda, Senegal, Swaziland, Tanzania, Uganda, Upper Volta, Zambia	18	52.94
Nongovernmental press does not exist: Central African Republic, Congo, Equatorial Guinea, Gabon, Guinea, Ivory Coast, Mali, Mauritania, Niger, Sierra Leone, Somalia, Sudan, Togo, Zaïre	14	41.18
Total	34	100

*Informants in these countries express a low level of consensus regarding the required posting of bonds for nongovernmental newspapers and magazines.

It is still notable that 90 percent of the 20 nations with elements of a nongovernmental press do not require posting of bonds. These nations range from Ethiopia, which avoids the need for bonds by present military censorship, to Botswana, which relies on self-restraint. "The people, journalists too, are very cautious and it is not often that things like that [sedition or libel] appear in our newspapers," wrote one Botswana journalist. [21]

Only Kenya and Gambia still require the posting of bonds in order to get permission to publish a nongovernmental newspaper. One journalist in Kenya added "Individual journalists must post bonds." [22] The continued requirement in Kenya appears to be left over from the colonial era. During British administration, a book and newspaper law required all publishers and printers to post a bond of £500 against the event of libel or seditious activity.

TABLE 4.8

Severity of Libel and Sedition Laws

	Number of Countries	Percentage of Total
Highly restrictive: Central African Republic, Ethiopia, Gabon, * Malawi, Mauritania, * Somalia, * Uganda, Zaïre*	8	23.53
Fairly restrictive: Dahomey, Gambia, Kenya, Liberia, Nigeria, Rwanda, Sudan, * Swaziland, Upper Volta	9	26.47
Not very restrictive: Botswana, Burundi, Cameroon, Chad, Congo, * Ghana, Senegal, Sierra Leone, * Tanzania, Zambia	10	29.41
No effect at all: Equatorial Guinea, * Guinea, * Ivory Coast, * Lesotho, Mali, * Niger, * Togo*	7	20.59
Total	34	100

*Countries with a wholly government-owned press.

LIBEL AND SEDITION LAWS

A common press control throughout the world involves libel and sedition laws. Every world nation has libel laws to protect individuals from press abuses, and most countries have sedition acts for national security purposes.

Independent black Africa is no exception, but it does become a matter of interest to assess the effect of these laws on the operation of the press. For example, are national libel and sedition laws perceived as highly restrictive on the press by informants in the 34 nations?

Informants from eight African nations, as noted in Table 4.8, are of the opinion that their laws are highly restrictive. Five of these nations—Central African Republic, Gabon, Mauritania, Somalia, and Zaïre—have a completely government-owned press but journalists still perceive the libel and sedition laws as highly restrictive.

Journalists in other nations with a wholly government-owned press, however, perceived libel and sedition laws as having no effect at all. They reasoned that a government press was already heavily controlled and so the chance of violating libel or sedition laws was small. These nations include Equatorial Guinea, Guinea, Ivory Coast, Mali, Niger, and Togo. As a Togoese representative said, it is practically impossible to sue a government newspaper and it is unthinkable that a government organ would violate sedition laws. [23]

Most nations with nongovernmental newspapers and magazines were perceived by informants as having somewhat restrictive libel and sedition laws. Nigeria is rated as "fairly restrictive" and one journalist wrote, "The libel laws amount to a chain around the hand of journalists wishing or courageous enough to do exposes of scandalous deals." [24] The same rating is given in Liberia, where broadly worded libel and sedition laws make dangerous any but laudatory comment on political issues or figures.

Ethiopia and Malawi, although having aspects of a nongovernmental press, were rated "highly restrictive" by indigenous informants. Ethiopia's rating stems from a rather long and specific penal code that heavily restricts newspapers and magazines. Malawi owes its rating to President Banda, who has tightened libel and sedition laws in recent years. In July 1973, for example, he had the parliament (all members of the Malawi Congress Party) pass a law making the publication of a false report punishable by life imprisonment. Banda is the arbiter of whether a report is true or false.

NOTES

1. Area Handbook for the Democratic Republic of the Sudan, prepared by the Foreign Area Studies Program of the American University (Washington, D. C.: U. S. Government Printing Office, 1973), p. 214.
2. John C. Merrill and Ralph L. Lowenstein, Media Messages and Men (New York: David McKay, 1971), p. 196.
3. Donald Morrison et al., eds., Black Africa: A Comparative Handbook (New York: The Free Press, 1972), p. 93. The complete study appears in Jean Blondel, An Introduction to the Study of Comparative Government (New York: Praeger Publishers, 1970).
4. Comment on mail questionnaire from Nigeria, signed.
5. African Journalist, March 1972.
6. Letter from James F. Scotten, dean of the Institute of Mass Communications, Lagos, July 11, 1973.
7. Ildephonse Munyeshyaka, first secretary at the embassy of Rwanda, Washington, D. C., personal interview on January 11, 1974.
8. Comment on mail questionnaire from Ghana, signed.

9. Comment on mail questionnaire from Ethiopia, signed.

10. Comment on mail questionnaire from Liberia, signed.

11. B. M. Khaketla, Lesotho 1970–An African Coup Under the Microscope (Berkeley: University of California Press, 1972), p. 230.

12. Arnold Temu, University of Dar es Salaam, Tanzania, personal interview in April 1971.

13. John Hanson, "The Press in Liberia," master's thesis, Syracuse University, 1972, p. 82.

14. Area Handbook for Chad, prepared by the Foreign Area Studies Program of the American University (Washington, D. C.: U. S. Government Printing Office, 1972), p. 97.

15. Comment on mail questionnaire from Ghana, anonymous.

16. Ibid.

17. John Patrick Seawell, "Mass Communication in Ethiopia: Blunted Instrument of Government," master's thesis, University of Texas, 1971, p. 166.

18. Arthur Changawa, third secretary at the embassy of Kenya, Washington, D. C., personal interview on January 7, 1974.

19. Comment on mail questionnarie from Kenya, signed.

20. Comment on mail questionnaire from Cameroon, signed.

21. Comment on mail questionnaire from Botswana, signed.

22. Comment on mail questionnaire from Kenya, signed.

23. William Koffi Adjoyi, counselor at the embassy of Togo, Washington, D. C., personal interview on January 9, 1974.

24. Comment on mail questionnaire from Nigeria, signed.

5

BROADCASTING:
THE GOVERNMENT
MONOPOLY

Radio broadcasting probably is the most universal form of mass communication in independent black Africa. Cheap transistor radios have brought the spoken word to millions of rural Africans, and broadcasting has broken the barriers of illiteracy and poverty. Given Africa's great oral tradition, many observers feel that radio and television have already eclipsed print media as the continent's truly mass communication.

Table 5.1, compiled from press directories and crosschecked with primary sources, shows that all of black Africa's 34 nations have radio broadcasting facilities. Ghana, Liberia, Zaïre, and Nigeria lead the region with the most stations (facilities capable of originating programs), while countries like Botswana, Senegal, and Mali have one centralized station for the entire country. Mali's station, however, is the most powerful radio transmitter in West Africa, thanks to aid from the People's Republic of China. [1]

More than half of the black African nations also have television at present. This number is expected to rise in the near future as Cameroon, Dahomey, and Somalia complete plans to install television facilities. Dahomey, for example, has a pilot system being readied for experimental purposes. Equatorial Guinea already has a television station, but it has been inoperative since 1969. Cuban technicians began studying the facilities in early 1974, with the idea of reestablishing service in black Africa's newest and least populous country. [2]

Mainland Tanzania is one of the more prosperous nations that has no plans for establishing a television station. President Julius Nyerere considers television an unnecessary luxury that only the rich can afford. It should be noted, however, that an increasing number of television receivers are being found on the coastal area near Dar es Salaam because Zanzibar, part of the United Republic of Tanzania but having its own autonomy, has a television station.

Television, like radio, is distributed unevenly in the 18 nations that have systems. Ghana and Nigeria not only have multiple stations

TABLE 5.1

Radio and Television Facilities

Country	State-Owned Radio Stations	State-Owned TV Stations	Privately Owned Radio Stations[a]
Botswana	1	0	
Burundi	1	0	1
Cameroon	4	0	
Central African Republic	3	1	
Chad	3	0	
Congo	2	1	
Dahomey	4	0	
Equatorial Guinea	2	1[b]	
Ethiopia	5	1	1
Gabon	3	1	
Gambia	2	0	
Ghana	12	3	
Guinea	1	0	
Ivory Coast	2	1	
Kenya	1	1	
Lesotho	4	0	
Liberia	8	1	2
Malawi	1	0	
Mali	1	0	
Mauritania	1	0	
Niger	3	0	
Nigeria	6	5	
Rwanda	1	0	1
Senegal	1	1	
Sierra Leone	2	1	
Somalia	2	0	
Sudan	1	1	
Swaziland	2	0	
Tanzania	2	0[c]	
Togo	2	1	
Uganda	2	1	
Upper Volta	2	1	
Zaire	8	2	
Zambia	1	1	
Total	96	25	5

[a]Radio stations operated by Christian missions or foreign governments.

[b]The station in Equatorial Guinea is presently inoperative.

[c]A television station in Zanzibar reaches the coastal areas of Tanzania.

but also lead black Africa in the number of receivers. Ghana has at least 16, 000 sets and there are more than 50, 000 in Nigeria.[3] On the other hand, the Congo has 500 sets and the Central African Republic, which recently opened its station, has only 40 or 50 sets in the entire country.[4]

Although many African nations have nongovernmental newspapers and magazines, general audience broadcasting is exclusively state-owned in all 34 nations. Some nations, like Burundi, Ethiopia, Liberia, and Rwanda, have allowed religious organizations or foreign governments to operate ratio transmitters, but these stations serve specialized interests and do not make partisan comment on the social, political, and economic affairs of the host country.

Most if not all of the state-owned radio and television stations accept advertising from commercial interests as a source of revenue, but control and operation of these facilities remain firmly in government hands. Such ownership and control should be considered in the context of press-government relationships since access to broadcasting facilities and alternative programming, by nongovernmental interests, is restricted and curtailed.

The extent and degree of governmental control over broadcasting facilities can be indexed in several ways. This chapter assesses government control from the standpoint of (1) financial support, (2) the individual or group directly responsible for policy formulation, and (3) the criteria for the selection and employment of broadcasting personnel.

MAJOR SOURCES OF BROADCASTING FUNDS

Since all broadcasting facilities in black Africa are state-owned, it is not surprising that current governments also are primarily responsible for funding such operations. Table 5.2 shows that more than a third of the nations include funding in their national budgets while another 20 nations finance broadcasting through budgetary allocations from the ministry of information or a similar agency.

Although it can be argued that both sources represent governmental funding and influence, they do represent subtle differences in the type of control that can be exerted. It is suggested that monies allocated through national budgets give the prime minister or president direct control over the nature of broadcasting services. Budgetary allocations from the ministry of information, however, shift some of this power to a cabinet minister and decentralize the control of broadcasting within the government.

The lack of private enterprise and the poverty of most African countries limit revenues from commercial advertising. Of the 18 nations

TABLE 5.2

Major Sources of Broadcasting Funds

	Number of Countries	Percentage of Total
Subsidy from general government funds: Burundi, * Congo, Dahomey, Equatorial Guinea, Gambia, * Guinea, Malawi, Mali, Mauritania, Nigeria, * Rwanda, Senegal*	12	35.29
Budgetary allocation from ministry of government: Botswana, Cameroon, Central African Republic, * Chad, Ethiopia, Gabon, * Ghana, Ivory Coast, * Kenya, Lesotho, Sierra Leone, Somalia, Sudan, Swaziland, Tanzania, Togo, * Uganda, Upper Volta, Zaïre, Zambia	20	58.83
Commercial advertising: Liberia, Niger*	2	5.88
Total	34	100

*Informants in these countries express a low consensus regarding the major source of operating funds for broadcasting.

that have some commercial advertising, only Liberia and Niger have large enough advertising revenues to be somewhat independent of government funding. Other nations generating a degree of commercial advertising revenue, according to informants, include Ghana, Ivory Coast, Kenya, Lesotho, Nigeria, Senegal, and Tanzania.

The fact remains, however, that most stations are financed directly by the state. One observer wrote, "Advertising is accepted but is usually so low that programmes can never be free from the accusing gaze of a government official."[5]

Another form of revenue involves license fees on radio and television sets. A number of nations have such fees, but none count on the revenue to substantially finance broadcasting. Loans from foreign governments are uncommon; only the Central African Republic and Equatorial Guinea have major foreign loans for broadcasting operations at the present time.

DIRECT CONTROL OF BROADCASTING

The administrative structure of broadcasting operations in African
countries gives some insight into the degree of control that can be
exerted.

Many nations in Western Europe, including the former colonial
powers of England, Belgium, and France, utilize relatively autonomous
public corporations to insulate broadcasting from political pressures
exerted by the political parties currently in power. The British, in particular, introduced the concept to Africa, but a decade of independence
has shown that the idea was not widely accepted.

Rosalynde Ainslie, writing in 1966, perceived the trend:

> African broadcasting . . . tends away from the concept
> of broadcasting as a function independent of government, such
> as was envisaged by the British . . . in colonial days. The
> tasks of radio have emerged as so much part of, and essential
> to, the policies of government, that many of the countries that
> inherited with independence a statutory corporation in charge
> of broadcasting, have legislated to bring radio and television
> back under direct ministerial control. [6]

Today, in independent black Africa, relatively autonomous public
corporations for radio broadcasting are nonexistent. Even state-owned
corporations with board of directors that include nongovernmental members are rarities. Only three nations—Ghana, Nigeria, and Liberia—
still claim this type of organization, as shown in Table 5.3.

Kenya and Tanzania were once in this category, but steps were
taken in the mid-1960s to dissolve statutory corporations and place
radio services directly under the ministry of information or a similar
agency. Until 1973, Malawi also had a government corporation with
a diverse board of directors that included educators, chiefs, businessmen, government officials, and party members. [7] The Malawi Broadcasting Corporation, however, now exists in name only because
President Banda has disbanded the Ministry of Information and taken
direct control of all broadcasting activities. [8]

Of the three nations that do have full-fledged corporations with
somewhat independent and diverse boards of directors, Nigeria probably is the best example. The Nigerian Broadcasting Corporation was
established in 1956 and continues to operate in a highly professional
and efficient manner with little interference from the current military
government. It does, however, receive the majority of its operating
funds from government allocation. [9]

The status of the government corporation in Ghana is less certain
since Colonel Ignatius Acheamong and the National Redemption Council

TABLE 5. 3

Control of Radio Broadcasting

	Number of Countries	Percentage of Total
Head of government: Central African Republic, Chad, Equatorial Guinea, Malawi	4	11. 77
Government minister: Botswana, Burundi, * Cameroon, Dahomey, Ethiopia, Gabon, * Gambia, Ivory Coast, * Kenya, Lesotho, Mali, Mauritania, Niger, * Rwanda, * Senegal, * Sierra Leone, Somalia, Sudan, Swaziland, Tanzania, Togo, * Uganda, Upper Volta, Zaïre, Zambia	25	73. 53
State-owned corporation: Ghana, Liberia, Nigeria	3	8. 82
Majority political party: Congo, * Guinea	2	5. 88
Total	34	100

*Informants in thes countries express a low level of consensus regarding the direct control of radio broadcasting.

took power in 1972. For example, it has been reported that the Ministry of Information exerts a major influence in the affairs of the corporation. Liberia's radio corporation does not receive direct budgetary allocations, but grants are given in the form of payment for broadcasting public announcements. [10]

The fact remains, however, that three-fourths of the nations in Africa have opted for radio broadcasting directly under the ministry of information or a similar agency. Although such a situation provides for more efficient management in terms of coordinating national plans and diffusing information about them, it also means that radio is more rigidly controlled and access is limited to government spokesmen.

It does not appear that there will be any shift in the structure of radio services under a ministry of information. Zambia and Somalia once considered the establishment of a relatively autonomous corporation but apparently have abondoned the idea. In Somalia, such a corporation was viewed as having four major values: (1) more efficient operations, (2) freer financial transactions, (3) better possiblity for revenues, and (4) higher reliability and credibility. [11]

Table 5.4 summarizes the administrative structure of television operations in black Africa. Again, about three-fourths of the 18 nations with television have a government minister in direct charge of the system. As in radio broadcasting, only Ghana, Liberia, and Nigeria have government-organized corporations with directors representing various segments of national life. The Liberian system, for example, is under the Telecommunications Commission and is expected to provide its own financing through commercial advertising and license fees. [12]

SELECTION OF BROADCASTING PERSONNEL

In most black African nations, government ministers have direct responsibility for administration and overall policy formulation of national broadcasting services. It also is important to review the training and employment category of the personnel responsible for the daily operation of radio and television facilities.

The electronic media in black Africa are rapidly becoming professionalized as increasing numbers of employees receive regular training. Much of the training, however, is still conducted abroad due to the paucity of qualified instruction in Africa. Table 5.5 shows that over 90 percent of the African nations now have the daily operation of broadcasting in the hands of local personnel trained abroad.

At least 15 of these nations also utilize instruction within the country, but not to the same extent as Burundi and Ethiopia. Local teachers usually have been trained abroad or are foreign expatriates on contract.

It is obvious that the reliance on foreign technicians in the early years of independence has considerably diminished. Only Gabon still uses a large percentage of expatriates. Central African Republic, Chad, Congo, and Zambia also utilize foreign technicians, but to a lesser extent.

From the standpoint of control, it also is encouraging that officials of the current government or majority political party are not involved in the daily broadcasting operations. If they are, it is because of specialized training in the field. One Ethiopian informant noted, for example, "Local personnel trained abroad and officials of the current government are one and the same. "[13]

Table 5.6 indicates that the reservoir of trained broadcasting personnel tends to remain, regardless of political instability or changes in government. Broadcasting employees are considered civil service employees in at least 20 countries. In another four nations—Ghana,

TABLE 5.4

Control of Television Operations

	Number of Countries	Percentage of Total
Head of government: Central African Republic, Equatorial Guinea	2	5.88
Government minister: Ethiopia, Gabon,* Ivory Coast,* Kenya, Senegal,* Sierra Leone,* Sudan, Togo, Uganda, Upper Volta, Zaïre, Zambia	12	35.29
State-owned corporation: Ghana, Liberia, Nigeria	3	8.83
Majority political party: Congo*	1	2.94
No television system: Botswana, Burundi, Cameroon, Chad, Dahomey, Gambia, Guinea, Lesotho, Malawi, Mali, Mauritania, Niger, Rwanda, Somalia, Swaziland, Tanzania	16	47.06
Total	34	100

*Informants in these countries express a low consensus regarding the direct control of television facilities.

Liberia, Malawi, and Nigeria—broadcasting employees are paid and hired by government corporations.

Nine African countries consider broadcasting personnel as employees of the current government. Consequently, they are subject to dismissal if the government changes policy or leadership. In such a situation, it is more likely that personnel will make every effort to show loyalty and support the current ruling elite.

The increasing professionalization of broadcasting in Africa also is expressed in emphasis on training as a criterion for the appointment of broadcasting executives. Informants in more than half the African nations now say professional training is the major criterion. Of course, this is not to say that political considerations and other criteria are not also considered.

TABLE 5.5

Daily Operation of Broadcasting Facilities

	Number of Countries	Percentage of Total
Local personnel trained abroad:	31	91.18
Botswana,* Cameroon, Central African Republic,* Chad,* Congo,* Dahomey,* Equatorial Guinea, Gambia,* Ghana, Guinea, Ivory Coast,* Kenya, Lesotho, Liberia, Malawi, Mali, Mauritania, Niger, Nigeria, Rwanda, Senegal, Sierra Leone, Somalia, Sudan,* Swaziland,* Tanzania, Togo, Uganda, Upper Volta, Zaïre, Zambia		
Local personnel trained at home:	2	5.88
Burundi,* Ethiopia		
Foreign technicians: Gabon*	1	2.94
Total	34	100

*Informants in these countries express a low consensus regarding the nature of personnel in charge of daily broadcasting activities.

TABLE 5.6

Employment of Broadcasting Personnel

	Number of Countries	Percentage of Total
Employed by current government:	9	26.47
Burundi, Central African Republic, Congo,* Equatorial Guinea, Niger,* Rwanda,* Somalia,* Swaziland, Togo*		
Employed by civil service: Botswana,	20	58.82
Cameroon, Chad,* Dahomey, Ethiopia, Gabon, Gambia, Ivory Coast, Kenya, Lesotho, Mali, Mauritania, Senegal, Sierra Leone, Sudan, Tanzania, Uganda, Upper Volta, Zaïre, Zambia		
Employed by government corporation:	4	11.77
Ghana, Liberia, Malawi, Nigeria		
Employed by majority political party:	1	2.94
Guinea		
Total	34	100

*Informants in these countries express a low consensus regarding the employment classification of broadcasting personnel.

TABLE 5.7

Major Criterion in Appointment of Broadcast Executives

	Number of Countries	Percentage of Total
Professional training: Cameroon, Gambia, Ghana, Ivory Coast, Kenya, Lesotho,* Liberia, Mali, Niger, Nigeria, Rwanda, Senegal, Sierra Leone, Sudan, Tanzania,* Uganda, Upper Volta, Zambia	18	52.94
Past government service: Botswana, Burundi, Central African Republic, Dahomey,* Ethiopia, Swaziland	6	17.65
Leadership in majority political party: Congo, Equatorial Guinea, Gabon, Guinea, Togo,* Zaïre*	6	17.65
Insufficient information: Chad, Malawi, Mauritania, Somalia	4	11.76
Total	34	100

*Informants in these countries express a low level of consensus regarding the major criterion for appointment of broadcasting executives.

The emphasis on professional training is affected by other requirements in several nations. The military regime in Ghana appoints executives on the basis of merit and length of government service, but loyalty to the present leadership is another criterion. In Kenya, tribal affiliation plays a major role. A Nigerian informant also wrote, "Professional training is the most important but allegiance to government and friendships are strong."[14]

Table 5.7 shows that at least six nations still regard leadership in the majority political party as the main criterion for appointment of broadcasting executives. One informant in Equatorial Guinea merely noted that "loyalty to the head of state" was the sole criterion.[15] Another in Zaïre wrote, "Loyalty to the party."[16] Although there was insufficient consensus to classify Malawi, one informant wrote, "Nobody can get a job if he isn't a member in good standing with the Malawi Congress Party."[17]

Past government service is considered a major criterion in another six nations. In Ethiopia and Swaziland, this is manifested in past

loyal service to the monarch. It would appear that loyalty and support
of the current government are underlying themes in many African countries
despite the emphasis on training and qualifications.

NOTES

1. Colin Legum, ed., Africa Contemporary Record—Annual Survey
and Documents (New York: Africana, 1973), p. B655.
2. Letter from foreign diplomat who wishes to remain anonymous,
January 29, 1974.
3. UNESCO Statistical Yearbook (Paris: UNESCO Publications,
1972), p. 842.
4. "Lord High Everything," Time, March 4, 1974, p. 39.
5. Doug Crawford, "Africa's Airwaves: The Medium and the
Message," African Development, November 1969, p. 18.
6. Rosalynde Ainslie, The Press in Africa: Communications Past
and Present (New York: Walker, 1966), p. 174.
7. Rodwell M. K. Mbale, minister at the embassy of Malawi,
Washington, D. C., personal interview on January 3, 1974.
8. Africa Report, November-December 1973, p. 43.
9. Magaji Dambatta, counselor at the embassy of Nigeria in
Washington, D. C., personal interview on January 7, 1974.
10. Temynors Kla-Williams, press counselor at the embassy of
Liberia, Washington, D. C., personal interview on January 4, 1974.
11. Guy M. Roppa, "Communication for Modernization in a Nomadic
Society: Conditions and Prospects in Somalia," master's thesis,
Indiana University, 1970), p. 226.
12. Interview with Kla-Williams, January 4, 1974.
13. Comment on mail questionnaire from Ethiopia, signed.
14. Comment on mail questionnaire from Nigeria, anonymous.
15. Comment on mail questionnaire from Equatorial Guinea, anonymous.
16. Comment on mail questionnaire from Zaïre, signed.
17. Comment on mail questionnaire from Malawi, anonymous.

CHAPTER

6

RESTRAINTS ON
FOREIGN MEDIA

The previous chapters have documented the types of controls exerted on a country's local media. They indicate that government ownership and control is so pervasive in many black African nations that foreign media often serve as the only independent, nongovernmental source of information.

As an alternative, foreign periodicals can fulfill a function beyond their limited circulations. They often preserve what little press freedom exists in a country because the educated elites demand access to foreign newsmagazines, newspapers, and films. Many have studied abroad and insist on Le Monde or the Guardian as part of their daily routine. Such media permit them to keep up with world affairs, and often to find out what is happening in their own countries.

It is a form of selective press freedom, however, because few people in independent black Africa have the language proficiency and affluence to utilize foreign media. The combined circulations of Time and Newsweek, perhaps the most widely distributed newsmagazines in the world, total only 42,385 for the Anglophone African nations. [1]

Nigeria, with its 70 million citizens, accounts for 30 percent of this total, while the 360,000 citizens of tiny Gambia receive a total of 111 copies each week.

Despite the small circulations of Time, Newsweek, and other foreign periodicals, they do reach the literate elite and decision makers in business, industry, and government. However, this is not to say that foreign periodicals enjoy unhindered circulation in many African nations. Governments on occasion ban or confiscate newsstand copies to protect the "public order and safety." This usually happens when the offending newspaper or magazine carries a critical story about the nation's leaders or policies.

By the same token, government officials often attempt to restrict information directed outside the country. Foreign journalists may be denied entrance or required to file their outgoing cables with the government censor. This type of government control filters what the rest of the world hears and reads about the internal affairs of many African nations.

This chapter documents the extent of control that African officials exert on incoming foreign media and the outgoing flow of news. It considers (1) censorship of foreign entertainment films, (2) the countries that have banned or confiscated foreign publications in the past two years, (3) visa requirements for foreign journalists, (4) government policies regarding the cabling of stories outside the country, and (5) restraints on the flow of international news within the country.

CENSORSHIP OF FOREIGN ENTERTAINMENT FILMS

Independent black Africa, more than any other region in the world, must rely on foreign-produced films for cinema entertainment. The film industry is just beginning in Africa, and only a few full-length features are produced in any one year. Most of this limited production has been centered in Senegal, Ivory Coast, and Nigeria. [2]

The foreign films originate from many countries. The small Asian communities of East Africa are fond of Indian films while English-speaking Africans prefer British and American films. Francophone Africa relies heavily on French films while other nations, because of ideology, utilize films supplied by the Communist bloc nations.

The cinema, like the other mass media in Africa, is concentrated in urban areas. There still are few mobile vans to take films to the rural populations, which often constitute 90 percent or more of a nation's citizens. Mauritania, for example, has only one indoor theater with 500 seats for a total national population of one million. [3] In more urbanized nations of Africa, like Ghana and Nigeria, weekly cinema attendance numbers several hundred thousand.

Reliance on foreign entertainment films has led to charges by Herbert Schiller and others that the cinema is a form of cultural imperialism. Africans are bombarded with foreign cultural values and lifestyles that have little relevance to their own lives. In addition, it is feared that films from more industrialized nations raise the frustration level of Africans who do not have automobiles, large houses, or even electricity.

These charges and fears have some value from a socialization standpoint. Consequently, most African governments have attempted to screen foreign entertainment films for upsetting material before they are released for public viewing. Table 6.1 shows that there is some form of formalized government preview of foreign films in over 90 percent of the black African nations.

TABLE 6.1

Government Censorship of Foreign Films

	Number of Countries	Percentage of Total
Review of films before public release: Burundi, Cameroon, Central African Republic, Chad, Congo, Dahomey, Equatorial Guinea, Ethiopia, Gabon, Gambia,* Ghana, Guinea, Ivory Coast, Kenya, Liberia, Malawi, Mali, Mauritania, Niger, Nigeria, Senegal, Sierra Leone, Somalia, Sudan, Swaziland, Tanzania, Togo, Uganda,* Upper Volta,* Zaïre, Zambia	31	91.18
No review of films before public release: Botswana,* Lesotho, Rwanda*	3	8.82
Total	34	100

*Informants in these countries express a low level of consensus regarding governmental screening of foreign entertainment films before public release.

The screening of films usually takes two forms. The most pervasive censorship is based on concepts of morality and violence. Nudity, long embraces, bedroom scenes, erotic behavior, and even the wearing of miniskirts may be snipped out of a foreign film. The Kenyan censorship board, for example, banned "The Learning Tree" and "Women in Love" during 1971; authorities considered the former "inimical to racial harmony" while the second was considered sexually suggestive. The board's ruling, however, was overruled by the attorney general, who complained that the board of censorship was senile and "some of them haven't been out of Kenya for 50 years."[4] He also implied that the nineteenth-century morality of Christian missionaries might be somewhat dated.

Violence also is subject to deletion in foreign films because many government officials fear it agitates the audience. Graphic portrayal of murder, rape, or mayhem is taboo, as are scenes that show Europeans repulsing "a horde of attacking African savages." Upper Volta is particularly concerned about violence in films. According to one informant, a fight once broke out in a movie theater after the showing of a war film, and on another occasion several children fell to their deaths when they attempted to imitate the activities of Superman.[5]

Although sexual matters and violence are subject to the censor's scissors, many nations also have standards for political content. The Congo, for example, exercises rigid censorship on all foreign films that deviate from Marxist philosophy. Many films, according to one government spokesman, were "a torrent of cinematic filth" and contradicted the nation's social approach. [6] In Guinea, the council of censorship reviews films and educational content to assure that the socialist philosophy is presented in the right light. [7]

Ethiopia's censorship commission also is concerned about the political implications of films. The guideline was to prohibit material that would reflect negatively on the emperor or the Ethiopian Orthodox Church. [8] Consequently, films were not shown if they made reference, directly or indirectly, to politically sensitive topics. Similar censorship takes place in Tanzania, Uganda, and Sierra Leone.

Only three nations—Botswana, Lesotho, and Rwanda—indicate that there is no formal censorship mechanism for the screening of foreign films. But in Botswana and Lesotho, the films are provided by South African distributors. As a result, the films already have been censored by the South African government on the basis of morality, violence, politics, and racial considerations.

CONFISCATION AND BANNING OF FOREIGN PERIODICALS

The lack of a diverse, well-developed press in independent black Africa has created a healthy market for foreign newspapers and magazines among the educated elites of the 34 nations. These elites, speaking either French or English, rely heavily on the publications of former colonial powers for news and information. Time and Newsweek also have an impact, as do pan-African publications like Drum and Jeune Afrique.

These newspapers and magazines often are the only source of nongovernmental information in a country, and it is important to document their relative freedom to circulate. In general, foreign media are not subject to the same strictures as local media. One reason is the content, which usually deals with issues outside the country. Yet government officials have seen fit to ban or confiscate foreign publications in 65 percent of the black African nations during the past two years (see Table 6.2).

Foreign newspapers and magazines are banned or seized for a variety of reasons, but political considerations are the most prevalent. This is particularly true when the offending publication has a critical or unflattering story about the particular nation.

Afrique Nouvelle of Dakar, before it suspended publication for financial reasons, was banned in Dahomey because of a "tendentious"

TABLE 6.2

Confiscation and Banning of Foreign Periodicals

	Number of Countries	Percentage of Total
Foreign periodicals banned or confis-cated in 1972-73: Cameroon, Central African Republic, Chad, Congo, Dahomey, Equatorial Guinea, Ethiopia, Gabon, Guinea, Ivory Coast,* Lesotho,* Malawi, Mali, Nigeria, Senegal, Sierra Leone,* Somalia, Sudan, Togo, Uganda, Zaïre, Zambia*	22	64.71
No foreign periodicals banned or confis-cated in 1972-73: Botswana, Burundi, Gambia, Ghana, Kenya, Liberia,* Mauritania, Rwanda, Swaziland, Tanzania, Upper Volta*	11	32.35
Insufficient information: Niger	1	2.94
Total	34	100

*Informants in these countries express a low level of consensus regarding incidents of confiscation or banning in 1972-73.

article about that nation's most recent military coup.[9] Ethiopia occa-sionally has banned Time and Newsweek when articles did not compli-ment the nation's foreign and domestic policies. This also has occurred in Malawi when British newspapers contained articles touching on internal affairs. In Zaïre, one informant wrote, "In the past year, one issue of Newsweek was held back from circulation when it carried an article considered offensive to President Mobutu."[10]

In most cases, only specific issues of foreign newspapers or magazines have been banned or seized. Some nations, however, have totally banned a particular publication. In December 1973, for example, General Idi Amin of Uganda banned Kenyan newspapers from circulating in Uganda. He said the Sunday Post, Sunday Nation, Daily Nation, and East African Standard were supporting "imperialists, Zionists and colo-nialists."[11] Equatorial Guinea has a law against the importation of any newspapers from its former colonial master, Spain. The Rhodesian Herald and various South African publications have been banned in Malawi since 1972.

At least 11 African nations have not banned or confiscated any foreign newspapers of magazines in the past two years. The list includes Kenya, which allows relatively free circulation of independent periodicals but does ban political tracts and newspapers from Communist countries. Foreign periodicals also circulate in Tanzania without hindrance, but all copies must be processed through the State Trading Corporation. This opens a possibility for censorship before distribution, but the primary purpose of the trading corporation is to regulate and conserve foreign exchange.[12]

VISA REQUIREMENTS FOR FOREIGN JOURNALISTS

Most if not all black African nations require foreign visitors to have visas. In most cases, tourists are automatically issued visas for specified lengths of time. Foreign journalists, however, often are considered a different class of visitor and the requirements for obtaining a visa may be more complex.

Many national leaders, sensitive to how their country is portrayed in the international press, carefully screen journalists who apply for visas. They are interested in the type of articles the applicant has previously written and the kind of publication being represented. James Hoagland, a Washington Post columnist and reporter who toured Africa, wrote:

> Since most African countries still require foreign visitors to have visas, it is a simple matter for the offended official to see to it that anyone who dissents from the official view is refused entry or is expelled from the country.[13]

Restrictions on visas for foreign journalists, of course, inhibit and control the type of information the rest of the world receives. Some nations are infrequently covered in the world press simply because foreign journalists rarely get permission to visit the country. The Congo, for example, bans foreign journalists as a class. Guinea presently is not issuing tourist visas, to say nothing of permission for foreign journalists.

At least eight nations in independent black Africa have special visa requirements for foreign journalists (see Table 6.3). In most cases, the journalist must make formal application directly to the country's minister of information. In the case of Mauritania, embassies are permitted to issue visas for journalists, but the general precaution is to check with the country's minister of information.

Fortunately, special visa requirements are not common in Africa. Russell Warren Howe, a long-time foreign correspondent who has covered many nations on the continent, wrote:

TABLE 6.3

Visa Requirements for Foreign Journalists

	Number of Countries	Percentage of Total
Foreign journalists require special permission to enter country: Congo, Equatorial Guinea, Guinea, Malawi, Mauritania, Sudan,* Uganda, Zaïre	8	23.53
Foreign journalists processed same way as other visitors: Botswana, Cameroon, Central African Republic, Dahomey, Ethiopia, Gabon, Gambia, Ghana, Ivory Coast, Kenya, Lesotho, Liberia, Mali, Niger, Nigeria,* Rwanda, Senegal, Sierra Leone, Somalia, Swaziland, Tanzania, Togo, Upper Volta	23	67.65
Insufficient information: Burundi, Chad, Zambia	3	8.82
Total	34	100

*Informants in these countries express a low level of consensus regarding visa requirements for foreign journalists.

Although from time to time I have faced intolerant attitudes from colonial or colonial type governments, in 11 years
on the continent only one African government has refused me
a visa. In this area, Black Africa's record probably compares
favorably with Asia and Latin America.[14]

Table 6.3 shows that 23 African nations, two-thirds of the total,
treat foreign journalists the same as other visitors in terms of visa
applications. The Central African Republic closely questions photo-
journalists at the arrival point; Zaïre is leery of television cameramen
but has no formalized restrictions on journalists seeking to enter the
country. Tanzanian officials also closely question a foreign visitor if
he states that he is a journalist on his visa application.

The general pattern in Africa is for foreign journalists to present
their credentials at the ministry of information or a similar government
agency after they enter the country. Nations like Cameroon, Ghana,

Kenya, Lesotho, Liberia, Rwanda, and Tanzania all require government approval of a journalist's activities in the country. This is particularly true if the journalist wishes to interview government officials and average citizens.

Nigeria is listed as having no special visa requirements for foreign journalists, but this only is a recent development. During most of 1973, the government had rigid regulations for journalists who wanted to visit the country. Embassies were instructed to compile a dossier on the applicant's political views, the purpose of the visit, the type of information desired, and the political orientation of the publication.

The Nigerian government of General Yakubu Gowon imposed such restrictions on visa applications because of a feeling that too many critical articles had been appearing in the foreign press. The government had been cool to newsmen since the Biafran civil war, during which many correspondents wrote articles considered sympathetic to the secessionist viewpoint. In 1973, for example, reporters for the Washington Post and the Times of London were denied visas to visit Nigeria.

Nigerian diplomatic sources now indicate that visa restrictions on foreign journalists ended in December 1973. Embassies, however, are still instructed to exercise prudence in granting visas to journalists. [15]

Although there was insufficient information to categorize Zambia, one informant wrote, "Journalists are regarded as different from tourists."[16]

SUBMISSION OF CABLES FOR GOVERNMENT APPROVAL

The information indicates that few African nations attempt to impose special visa requirements on foreign correspondents. Even fewer require journalists to submit cables for government approval before they are sent.

Only three nations—Congo, Equatorial Guinea, and Guinea—presently require review of cables sent by foreign correspondents. There is some evidence that Malawi and Somalia censor outgoing cables, but the information is inconclusive. One informant in Malawi, for example, wrote, "You can't send cables except by the back door, of course."[17] Other informants disagreed.

At any rate, in recent years fewer nations have required review of cables. In mid-1967, for example, General Yakubu Gowon of Nigeria issued a decree prohibiting foreign correspondents from publishing or relaying anything detrimental to the federal government. Zaïre, in the following year, also issued a regulation that all correspondents must submit cables to local authorities. Sudan has fluctuated on the issue in recent years. Some correspondents have been censored while others have been free to send cables. One Liberian wrote that Time magazine correspondents occasionally have difficulties in sending cables.

The censorship of outgoing cables, however, is now relatively rare in independent black Africa. Table 6.4 shows that 85 percent of the nations have no official policy on review of outgoing news stories.

But several questions remain. The threat of censorship, despite the official policy, may still exist because telecommunications facilities are universally owned and operated by the government. One journalist in the Ivory Coast wrote, "All copy, even from local representatives of international wire services, goes through the post office and can be stopped there. This has happened once in the last two and a half years."[18]

African governments also may have abandoned formal censorship of cables after finding it relatively ineffective. For foreign correspondents, faced with the prospect of censorship, may simply wait to file their stories after they leave the country.

Consequently, many African governments have discovered the more potent weapon of expelling journalists. The cables of Agence France-Presse (AFP) in the Central African Republic have never been censored, but three of the agency's correspondents have been expelled in recent years.[19] Chad also expels AFP correspondents on a regular basis. In Uganda, several British journalists have been deported since General Idi Amin took power in 1971. One journalist, David Martin of the London Observer, even has a price on his head for reporting the death of an American journalist and a British sociologist who were investigating reports of mass killings by Uganda's army.[20]

Kenya also has been known to force the departure of journalists. Philip Short, a reporter for the London Times and BBC, was expelled in 1973. No reason was given. And in Malawi, in August 1974, President Banda banned all foreign journalists from the country.

EXCLUSIVE CONTRACTUAL AGREEMENTS FOR FOREIGN NEWS

It already has been documented that almost two-thirds of the African nations exercise some control over the incoming flow of foreign newspapers and magazines. Specific issues are seized on occasion, while other publications are completely banned.

International news also is provided by the international news agencies. Table 6.5 however, shows that this medium is even more rigidly controlled than the circulation of foreign periodicals. Of the African governments, 70 percent have exclusive contracts with international news agencies. This means that the national news agency or a similar governmental office receives all incoming foreign news and then distributes it to the local media.

TABLE 6.4

Submission of Cables for Government Approval

	Number of Countries	Percentage of Total
Foreign journalists required to submit cables: Congo, Equatorial Guinea, Guinea	3	8.82
Foreign journalists free to cable without official permission: Botswana, Burundi, Cameroon, Central African Republic, Chad, Dahomey, Ethiopia, Gabon, Gambia, Ghana, Ivory Coast, Kenya, Lesotho, Liberia, Mali, Mauritania, Niger, Nigeria, Rwanda, Senegal, Sierra Leone, Sudan, Swaziland, Tanzania, Togo, Uganda, Upper Volta, Zaïre, Zambia	29	85.30
Insufficient information: Malawi, Somalia	2	5.88
Total	34	100

Such an arrangement in 24 nations gives the government unlimited power to filter, screen, and control the public's knowledge of events abroad. News items can be edited, changed, or deleted to suit the government's foreign and domestic policies. The other danger of exclu-contracts with international news services is the feeling by many newsmen that a wire service cannot maintain objectivity and independence when its principal client in a country is the government.

In many cases, the government's control of incoming foreign news is merely an extension of its ownership and operation of all media. This is true in at least 14 nations on the list. The other consideration is economic. Many individual newspapers cannot afford the services of an international news agency, so the government purchases and distributes the service at reduced cost.

Such econimic considerations are reasons for the exclusive contractual agreements in Ghana, Liberia, and Somalia. One Ghanaian informant stated, "It helps save foreign currency."[21] In Liberia, a journalist wrote, "Exclusive contracts are more for economic reasons than government policy."[22] When Somalia nationalized its press, the

TABLE 6. 5

Exclusive Government Contracts
with Foreign News Agencies

	Number of Countries	Percentage of Total
Government has exclusive contract with foreign news agencies: Burundi, Cameroon, Central African Republic, Chad, Congo, Dahomey, Equatorial Guinea, Ethiopia, Gabon, Ghana, Guinea, Ivory Coast, Liberia, Mali, Mauritania, Niger, Rwanda, Senegal, Sierra Leone, Somalia, Sudan, Togo, Upper Volta, Zaïre	24	70. 59
Privately owned media may contract with foreign news agencies: Botswana, Gambia, Kenya, * Lesotho, Nigeria, Swaziland, Tanzania, Uganda, Zambia	9	26. 47
Insufficient information: Malawi	1	2. 94
Total	34	100

*The Kenya News Agency has an exclusive contract with Reuters and United Press International (UPI) but newspapers are permitted to contract for the services of other international news agencies .

high cost of individual subscriptions to news services was described as one obstacle to the development of an independent press. [23]

At least three-fourths of the 24 nations with exclusive contracts have official national news agencies to receive the information. In most cases, the national news agency is a department at the ministry of information. The agency not only handles distribution of foreign news but also serves as the focal point of all national news. The concept of an independent news agency for newspapers and broadcasters—such as Reuters, Associated Press, United Press International, or even SAPA of South Africa—is nonexistent in independent black Africa.

The Ethiopian News Agency (ENA) is a good example of how the national news agencies in black Africa control virtually all national and international information in the country. One American scholar noted:

The discretionary power over the release of news, both domestic and foreign, which the ENA has—and exercises—must be appreciated. All incoming news is funneled into the information services section in Addis Ababa, where a decision is made to relay, alter and relay, or kill the item. [24]

Sierra Leone, which has no national news agency, distributes news by its Government Information Services. According to an official publication, "All releases and announcements put out by government, public corporations, commercial houses and charitable organizations are channeled to the public by the news media through this service." [25] In such a situation, it would be difficult for any news story to appear unless it had the approval of government officials.

About a fourth of the nations in black Africa (nine countries) permit independently owned newspapers to contract individually for the services of an international news agency. However, this is only theory in some countries since many struggling newspapers cannot afford the luxury of a teletype machine. Also, many are weeklies and have no real need for a daily wire service. In such a situation, it is more practical to rely on foreign news supplied by the government.

Kenya has an interesting variation. Reuters and United Press International (UPI) are received exclusively by the Kenya News Agency. Individual newspapers, however, are free to receive the Associated Press (AP) and Agence France-Presse (AFP) in their offices. Nigeria, on the other hand, has no national news agency and each daily newspaper is responsible for obtaining its own national and international news.

NOTES

1. Fritz Feuereisen and Ernst Schmacke, The Press in Africa (Munich: Verlag Dokumentation, 1973), pp. 260-63.

2. Film producers in Dakar and Abidjan, personal interviews held during April 1971.

3. William A. Hachten, Muffled Drums (Ames: Iowa State University Press, 1971), p. 283.

4. IPI Report, February 1971.

5. Dominique B. Sisso, counselor at the embassy of Upper Volta, Washington, D. C., personal interview on January 11, 1974.

6. The Official Associated Press Almanac for 1973 (New York: Almanac, 1972), p. 659.

7. Fouroumo Kourouma, counselor at the embassy of Guinea, Washington, D. C., personal interview on January 4, 1974.

8. John Patrick Seawell, "Mass Communication in Ethiopia: Blunted Instrument of Government," master's thesis, University of Texas, 1971, p. 163.

9. Colin Legum, ed. Africa Contemporary Record—Annual Survey and Documents 1972-73 (New York: Africana, 1973), p. B583.

10. Comment on mail questionnaire from Zaïre, signed.

11. The African Journalist, December 1973, p. 4.

12. Ministry of Information employee, Dar es Salaam, personal interview in April, 1971.

13. James Hoagland, "Censoring Stories: African Style," Washington Post, March 28, 1972.

14. Russell Warren Howe, "Reporting From Africa: A Correspondent's View," Journalism Quarterly 43 (Summer 1966): 316.

15. Magaji Dambatta, counselor at the embassy of Nigeria, Washington, D. C., personal interview on January 7, 1974.

16. Comment on mail questionnaire from Zambia, signed.

17. Comment on mail questionnaire from Malawi, signed.

18. Comment on mail questionnaire from Ivory Coast, signed.

19. Comment on mail questionnaire from Central African Republic, signed.

20. Michael Robbins, professor of anthropology at the University of Missouri, Columbia, personal interview on February 14, 1973. (Dr. Robbins had just returned from a research trip to Uganda.)

21. Comment on mail questionnaire from Ghana, signed.

22. Comment on mail questionnaire from Liberia, signed.

23. Guy M. Roppa, "Communication for Modernization in a Nomadic Society: Conditions and Prospects in Somalia," master's thesis, Indiana University, 1970, p. 211.

24. Seawell, "Mass Communication in Ethiopia," p. 161.

25. Republican Sierra Leone, pamphlet issued by Government Information Services, Freetown, p. 49.

7

THE EMERGING
PRESS PHILOSOPHY
OF BLACK AFRICA

An attempt to delineate and conceptualize the emerging press philosophies of independent black Africa confronts the researcher with a
complex array of variables and somewhat arbitrary decisions. Any
classification, no matter how well conceived, becomes a simplistic
conceptualization of complex social, political, and cultural forces
that have shaped the press differently in every nation.

Yet it is important from the standpoint of understanding to make
some effort at synthesizing the accumulated information. Although much
is left out in such a classification process, much also is gained in
terms of establishing the general patterns of press development in
black Africa.

The major danger in categorizing African nations, however, is the
tendency to rely on previously conceived theories of the press that
are based on Western values and concepts. All too often, we attempt
to force Third World nations into models of Western development and
experience.

E. Lloyd Sommerlad, an Australian journalist who has studied the
press in developing countries, wrote:

> It is inappropriate to judge governments and press in
> Africa by the same criteria one would apply in the United
> Kingdom or the United States . . . . Africa is in a transitional
> state, experimenting with new forms of democracy and building
> new political structures.
>
> In the West, the very idea of government publishing
> newspapers is anathema—it is incompatible with the indepen-
> dent, objective, critical role of a free press. But in the new
> nations, it is considered a logical and proper function of
> governments to produce newspapers, no different from con-
> ducting a broadcasting service which is widely recognized
> as falling within the area of public competence. [1]

It is for these reasons and others that the black African press cannot be adequately explained within the context of commonly accepted press philosophies. The best-known work is Four Theories of the Press by Siebert, Peterson, and Schramm, first published in 1956. This book, now in its fifth edition, was the first to deal adequately with four identified press philosophies—authoritarian, soviet communist, libertarian, and social responsibility. [2]

The authoritarian theory dates back to sixteenth-century England and is based on the concept that a privately owned press is rigidly controlled by the government through highly restrictive libel and sedition laws. Other methods of control include official permission to publish, prepublication censorship, seizure, and required posting of large bonds. The theory's major premise is the paramount importance of the state at the expense of individual liberties. It is negative in outlook; the objective is suppression of dissent rather than use of the press to positively promote national economic growth and a better standard of living.

Although the press in independent Africa has many elements of the authoritarian philosophy, as documented in previous chapters, many African nations cannot truly be classified as having such press systems. The theory emphasizes the existence of a privately owned but heavily controlled press. The more prevalent pattern in Africa, however, is for the government to own and operate the press.

Consequently, the soviet communist theory in some ways better describes the African setting. Like Russia, many African nations have a wholly owned government and party press, with major policy decisions made by a single ruling party. Many nations also put major emphasis on the positive harnessing of media outlets for the goals of national development and social change. Another ingredient in the almost mystical value placed on unity. In such a setting, the mass media become teachers of the masses.

But the soviet communist theory also is less than satisfactory to describe Africa. It is rooted in the ideology of Marx and Lenin and leaves out noncommunist nations that also utilize the press as an agent of national development. Although Guinea, Somalia, and Congo endorse selected concepts of communism, most African nations with a wholly owned government press express little or no ideological affinity for communism. Their press theory is based on economics and practical choice, not Western concepts of political ideology.

The libertarian theory also seems inappropriate for the nations of the Third World. It is based on the historical evolution of democratic concepts in Western Europe, which derived from universal literacy and the weakening of traditional monarchies. The basic foundation of the libertarian theory is a financially independent press that can operate as a watchdog on government. This theory can only be an ideal in Africa because there is still massive illiteracy and a lack of private capital to support an independent press.

TABLE 7.1

Dominant Ownership of Print Media

	Number of Countries	Percentage of Total
Ownership by government or ruling political party: Botswana, Burundi, Central African Republic, Chad, Congo, Dahomey, Equatorial Guinea, Ethiopia, Gabon, Ghana, Guinea, Ivory Coast, Malawi, Mali, Mauritania, Niger, Nigeria, Rwanda, Senegal, Sierra Leone, Somalia, Sudan, Tanzania, Togo, Upper Volta, Zaïre, Zambia	27	79.41
Ownership by private commercial interests: Cameroon, Gambia, Kenya, Lesotho, Liberia, Swaziland, Uganda	7	20.59
Ownership by multiple political parties:	0	0
Total	34	100

The final press theory offered in the Siebert-Peterson-Schramm analysis, social responsibility, is based on media responsibilities and functions in a highly urbanized, industrial society. Robert Hutchins and the Commission of Freedom of the Press (1947) were concerned about maintaining the free marketplace of ideas in an age when prohibitive costs restricted media ownership to only a few individuals or giant corporations. The commission suggested a degree of government control to assure that all viewpoints would have access to the mass media. Such a press theory, dealing with the problems of the mass media in post-industrial society, seems to have little relevance for the developing nations of Africa.

The social responsibility theory also is difficult to operationalize. Instead of emphasizing "freedom," it emphasizes "responsibility"— but what that means depends on who is defining it. John C. Merrill wrote, "Assuming that a nation's socio-political philosophy determines the press system, then it follows that every nation's press system is socially responsible."[3]

The failings and drawbacks of Four Theories of the Press were noted by William A. Hachten, who attempted to conceptualize another kind of press theory for the developing African nations. In his mind,

the press systems could be better organized by using three major concepts: neocommunist, authoritarian, and libertarian.

"Under the neocommunist ideology, all instruments of mass communication are brought under direct government control and ownership
so they may best serve government policy in a 'revolutionary state,'"
Hachten wrote.[4] The neocommunist theory, of course, is government
ownership and party control without the ideology of Marx or Lenin. But
the purpose of the press remains the same. As Hachten put it, "The
media must serve government, which is inseparable from the party and
its leader. The press should inform and work for national integration
and inspire the people, but not criticize the government or the leadership."[5]

Although he included libertarian as a classification, Hachten saw
little use for the category in Africa:

> The western model of the newspaper as a profit-making
> enterprise, independent of government, and supplying the
> public with reliable and objective news and public information
> is seldom found, although many African journalists aspire to
> such a press. Economic and social factors—poverty, illiteracy,
> economic structure, linguistic and ethnic diversity—have
> combined to inhibit such media development.[6]

However, Hachten said, the authoritarian classification has greater
application in independent black Africa:

> The non-governmental newspapers are usually permitted
> wide latitude to report the news, provide entertainment and
> pass along government information, as long as they do not
> directly challenge the government or its leadership. Some
> news media carry a good deal of news and even low level
> criticism of public officials. Yet always lurking behind the
> newsman is the potential restraint of government; the news-
> papers usually know how far to go.[7]

Hachten's press model, although interesting, is perhaps too simplistic. African press systems are either neocommunist or authoritarian
under his classification and there is little opportunity for more descriptive differentiation. Like the four theories discussed above, Hachten's
is also tied to press ownership in determining the difference between
neocommunist and authoritarian. It thus fails to recognize that wholly
owned governmental press systems can be more authoritarian than
neocommunistic.

A better model with a double approach is proposed by Ralph L.
Lowenstein. Press systems are classified on one level by ownership
and on another by press philosophy. Lowenstein's model is a two-tier

concept, which has more flexibility and descriptive quality than the
four theories or Hachten's model. The first tier is classification of
dominant press ownership in the country, using three categories:

> Private: Ownership by individuals or nongovernmental
> corporations, supported primarily by advertising or subscrip-
> tion.
> Multiparty: Ownership by competitive political parties,
> subsidized by party or party members.
> Government: Ownership by government or dominant govern-
> ment party, subsidized primarily by government funds or
> government-collected license fees. [8]

The second tier involves categorizing press philosophies:

> Authoritarian: Negative government controls over the
> press to stifle criticism and thereby maintain ruling elites.
> Social-Centralist: Positive government controls to
> harness the press for national economic and philosophical
> goals.
> Libertarian: Absence of government controls, assuring
> a free market place of ideas and operation of self-righting
> process.
> Social-Libertarian: Minimal government controls to unclog
> channels of communication and assure operational spirit of
> libertarian philosophy. All viewpoints, including those of
> the opposition, are heard.

Lowenstein's four press philosophies somewhat resemble Siebert-
Peterson-Schramm's four theories, but there are important differences.
For one, the soviet communist theory has been renamed the social-
centralist theory. In effect, this removes the ingredient of communist
ideology as a philosophical base and recognizes the fact that many
Third World nations harness the press for national development on the
basis of other considerations.

The social responsibility theory has been renamed social-libertarian concept by Lowenstein. The meaning is essentially the same
but avoids the semantic problem of attempting to define a socially
responsible press. As Merrill points out, it depends on who is doing
the defining: government or publishers. In the Third World, the social-
libertarian philosophy probably is best represented by nations that
provide an opportunity, through minimum controls, for political parties
to operate a press in opposition to the government in power.

By separating the element of ownership from the press philosophy,
Lowenstein's two-tier concept permits a different interpretation of
authoritarian press systems. The Siebert-Peterson-Schramm concept was

based on the premise that government controlled an essentially private press. In Africa, however, a nation may be authoritarian even though no privately owned press exists. The major criterion is not ownership but how the government utilizes its press system. In some African states, government ownership is a negative control because no attempt is made to harness the press for economic development. Government ownership and regulation are effective methods to suppress dissent, control the dissemination of information, and maintain the status quo; they may not be vehicles for social change.

By the same token, removal of ownership considerations makes it possible for nations with elements of a private press to be classified as having a social-centralist philosophy. Again, the emphasis is not necessarily on ownership but how national leaders view the role and function of the press. If the press (government or privately owned) is perceived as an integral part of national development, its role is defined within that cultural framework. This is particularly relevant when a private press operates under the watchful eyes of a military regime or a formalized one-party state.

It also is entirely possible, under Lowenstein's two-tier model, that different media in the country will reflect different ownerships and philosophies. The print media may be privately owned, operating under a social-libertarian philosophy, while the broadcasting services are government-owned and operate under the social-centralist philosophy. England is a good example.

Although the two-tier concept is not completely value-free in terms of Western judgments, it does offier a pragmatic and flexible system for classifying press systems in the Third World. Consequently, African informants were asked to classify their own nations on the two-tier concept of press ownership and philosophy.

On the matter of press ownership, they were asked how they would classify the dominant ownership of newspapers and magazines in their country. Broadcasting was eliminated from consideration because, without exception, it is government-owned and operated in Africa. In terms of press philosophy, informants were asked to summarize the government's official policy toward the press. In general, "press" in this context was interpreted as print media.

It should be pointed out that a brief description of each press philosophy was used—but without the labels of authoritarian, social-centralist, and so on, since it was felt that such labels might prejudice the respondents' answers. Individuals were asked to rank the following statements in order of importance:

The government should control the press to prevent any criticism that might threaten the stability of the national government. [Authoritarian concept.]

The government should actively harness the press to achieve national economic plans and unity. [Social-centralist concept.]

There should be an absence of government-involvement in the press because the public can adequately separate the truth from falsehoods in the press. [Libertarian concept.]

The government is obligated to assume minimum controls on the press to make sure all viewpoints, including those of the opposition, are heard. [Social-libertarian concept.]

Compilation of the informants' perceptions, it was hoped, would give the general pattern of press ownership and philosophy in each nation. The results were then checked for consistency with factual data about the press in the country, the current form of government, and recent political events. The general findings regarding press ownership and philosophy in independent black Africa are found in Tables 7.1 and 7.2.

PRESS OWNERSHIP

Independent Africa offers little diversity in terms of press ownership. Table 7.1 shows that nearly 80 percent of black Africa's 34 nations have a press predominantly owned by government or the ruling political party. It was initially thought that Nigeria, with its seven private dailies and many independent magazines, would not appear on the list, but Nigerian informants overwhelmingly perceived the Nigerian press as predominantly government-owned. The balance seems to have been tipped by the increasing proliferation of publications owned by state governments.

Only seven nations, less than a fourth of the total, were seen as having a press predominantly owned by private interests. Furthermore, informants in three of these nations—Gambia, Lesotho, and Liberia—expressed a low level of consensus, with a large minority considering their press as predominantly government-owned.

The third category, a press owned by political parties in opposition to each other, is nonexistent in black Africa. Upper Volta once qualified for this classification, but the military took over the reins of government again in February 1974. Prior to that date, several opposition parties were producing newsletters and newspapers, but all political activity is now suspended.

The general pattern of government press ownership in independent Africa comes as no surprise to experienced observers. Only the pervasive extent of government ownership—27 nations—is new.

TABLE 7.2

Press Philosophies in Black Africa

	Number of Countries	Percentage of Total
Authoritarian: Central African Republic, Chad, Congo, Dahomey, Equatorial Guinea, Ethiopia, Gabon, Lesotho, Malawi, Mali, Mauritania, Niger, Senegal, Sierra Leone, Somalia, Swaziland, Togo, Upper Volta, Zaïre	19	55.88
Social-centralist: Burundi, Cameroon, Ghana, Guinea, Ivory Coast, Nigeria, Rwanda, Sudan, Tanzania, Uganda, Zambia	11	32.35
Libertarian: Kenya	1	2.94
Social-libertarian: Botswana, Gambia, Liberia	3	8.83
Total	34	100

Although many of these nations have political and national ideology supporting a wholly government-owned press, one must also consider the economic factor. Most African nations, with high poverty and illiteracy, simply do not provide the setting for a privately owned press, which depends on commerical advertising and subscriptions. One Ghana informant wrote, "Private investment in the mass communications media is not forthcoming. It is only proper that government takes over from the private investors who left off."[9]

A Botswana journalist stated, "The dominant ownership is now governmental but it is a matter of finances instead of policy—a private paper would be allowed if it could finance itself and get enough readership."[10] Private enterprise in Nigeria, among all African nations, is probably in the best financial position to support an independent press. But Alhaji Babatunde Jose, chairman of the Daily Times group, considered it difficult even in Nigeria:

Another reason for government ownership of newspapers is that, with the exception of entrepreneurs like the Daily Times of Nigeria and the Ghana Graphic which were developed in

partnership between the Daily Mirror newspapers of London and
Nigerians, most other newspapers started by individuals or
organizations of Nigerians utterly lacked both financial
resources and management and technical know-how. [11]

The economic situation of independent black Africa is perhaps
best summarized by A. G. Fullerton of UNESCO in Dakar:

> there may be an economic as well as political explanation
> for the fact that the press in Africa tends to be government
> owned or operated. Take a typical West African country. A
> tiny proportion of the adult population (perhaps no more than
> 10 percent) is literate, and literate in French, not in the
> African languages, many of which do not yet have a written
> form. This elite tends to concentrate in the capital, with the
> exception of school teachers, agricultural extension workers
> and a few others in the villages. Newsprint is not available
> locally but must be imported from Canada or Scandinavia at
> prohibitive prices. The same is true for office equipment,
> printing machinery and everything else which goes into making
> a newspaper. A limited market on one hand and sky-high costs
> on the other may well mean that a commercial press is simply
> not viable economically. The only answer is a subsidized
> press, whether it be governmental or religious or whatever. [12]

There also is a feeling among African leaders that a private press
cannot satisfactorily meet the needs of a developing nation. Achieng
Oneko, Kenyan minister of information in the early years of nationhood,
once said:

> It is vitally important that every new nation should have
> government owned newspapers. This is because commerical
> newspapers aim primarily at making profits, so they are not
> likely to undertake the publication of newspapers for small
> linguistic groups. The government will have to fill the vacuum
> even if it means running the newspapers at a loss. [13]

A Nigerian journalist also indicated that a government-owned press
is the only viable solution for emerging Africa:

> The governments are steadily moving into the mass
> communications business since private enterprise has so
> far not been much of a success in the field. Indigenous private
> enterprise cannot fill the gap because of its lack of means.
> The religious groups and the political parties cannot fill it in
> view of their limited interests. And foreign private enterprise

cannot fill it either because of its lack of full commitment and
a consequent nationalist antagonism. [14]

Government ownership of the press also is related to the concept
of harnessing it for promotion of national development plans. Many
African nations see the press as playing an essential role in nation
building by creating a feeling of unity among peoples traditionally
divided by tribal loyalties. Another reason for government ownership,
according to several leaders, is the fact that most African societies
are in the midst of rapid change and an independent press would threaten
their precarious stability.

Other nations, like Tanzania, are developing along socialist lines
and all major industries are state-owned. In such a setting, Africans
argue, a privately owned press is not compatible with the nation's
political and economic philosophy. According to one college educator
in Tanzania, mass media as commercial enterprises are against the idea
of developing a socialist state. [15]

Yet a government-owned press has disadvantages in terms of credibility. In the words of English journalist Richard Hall:

> The essential failing of most official newspapers from the
> reader's point of view is that coverage of local affairs is always
> predictable. The editor is often a party man, with little know-
> ledge of journalism, who is hoping to use the job as a stepping
> stone. A cabinet split may be the talk of every bar in town, but
> nothing will appear in print until the editor can be sure of the
> outcome. Instead, there will be appeals for the public to ignore
> rumour-mongers and condemnation of disruptive elements—
> which each faction will take to be the other. [16]

PRESS PHILOSOPHY

Over half the nations in independent black Africa have an authoritarian press philosophy according to the compiled data, under Lowenstein's two-tier classification model. That is, negative government
controls are exerted over the press to stifle criticism and maintain the
current ruling political elite.

Eleven of the 19 nations with an authoritarian press philosophy
have a wholly government-owned press. They are included because
informants perceive the government's major objective as suppression
of dissent rather than harnessing the press in a positive way for national
economic and philosophical goals. Consequently, government ownership in these cases is viewed as a negative control.

The authoritarian nations have several forms of government. Nine are formal one-party states: Chad, Congo, Equatorial Guinea, Gabon, Malawi, Mauritania, Niger, Senegal, and Zaïre. Two are de facto one-party states: Lesotho and Sierra Leone. Another seven have military governments: Central African Republic, Dahomey, Ethiopia, Mali, Somalia, Togo, and Upper Volta. The remaining nation, Swaziland, is a monarchy. Mali and Swaziland are presently working on new constitutions that may change the form of government.

However, it would be unfair to simply close the discussion on nations in the authoritarian classification without some elaboration on the nations that seek to utilize the press in a positive way for national development (social-centralist concept). According to the African informants, at least half of the nations in the authoritarian classification have some emphasis on the press as having a role in national development.

These nations include Congo, Dahomey, Ethiopia, Gabon, Niger, Sierra Leone, Somalia, Togo, Upper Volta, and Zaïre. In Chad, for example, one informant wrote, "In Africa, the role of the journalist is to mobilize the masses around precise objectives."[17]

An Ethiopian diplomat said, "The press should improve the quality of education in the country."[18] An American scholar, however, said that the government has policies for harnessing the press but "they haven't done this."[19]

The press in Sierra Leone is charged with "unifying the country."[20] The role of the press in Togo supposedly is to "inform and form" and "mobilize the people behind the president and the party."[21] The same is true in Zaïre, where "the role of the journalist is to help educate the masses and rally support for the government."[22]

Table 7.2 shows that 11 nations (32 percent of the total) have a social-centralist philosophy; that is, the government's major policy is perceived as an attempt to harness the press to achieve national economic plans and unity. Again, most of the classifications reflect the perceptions and opinions of African correspondents in these nations.

Eight of the nations in the social-centralist concept have a mixed government and an operating private press. Only Guinea, Ivory Coast, and Sudan have a wholly government-owned press. It is interesting that five nations—Burundi, Ghana, Nigeria, Rwanda, and Uganda—have military governments. Another five—Cameroon, Guinea, Sudan, Tanzania, and Zambia—are formal one-party states. Ivory Coast is a de facto one-party state.

Nigeria, with its relatively well developed national and regional press, is under a military government, but most informants agree that the major emphasis of the Supreme Military Council is an active program of national development. The press (government and private) is expected to play a part in this program, and one observer noted: "Existing media are increasingly under pressure to temper criticisms, act 'constructively' and to promote developmental policies."[23]

In Rwanda, a diplomat said, "The role of the press is to inform and harness people for national development."[24] Sudan is pursuing national development along socialist lines and one informant reported, "The press is used by the government to promote and disseminate the socialist way of nation building."[25] Zambia's press philosophy is manifested in the responsibilities of journalists; one informant said, "We expect every sensible individual to reflect in his action interest in the development of Zambia."[26]

Although classified as social-centralist, almost half the nations exhibit overtones of the authoritarian press philosophy. Uganda is probably the best example. The remaining private newspapers in the country are heavily restricted and use much of their space to promote national development plans. They explicitly follow government policy, devoting much attention to interpreting General Amin's decrees (which often conflict with each other).

The major English-language daily, the Uganda Argus, became a government organ at the end of 1972 and was designated as the official organ for disseminating information about national development. Some observers note, however, that national development plans often take a back seat while the general builds a personality cult. The edition for the second anniversary of the republic contained 70 pictures; almost 60 percent of them were of General Amin.[27]

African informants also report that Cameroon, Guinea, Ivory Coast, and Sudan utilize the national press system to suppress dissent and maintain the ruling political elite.

Kenya is the only nation classified under the libertarian press philosophy. In general, there is an absence of government controls and the free marketplace of ideas concept is operational. Kenya also is the only country in black Africa where the government has left daily newspapers exclusively in private ownership.

The government, of course, prefers "constructive criticism" and press support for national development, but most Kenyan informants generally agree with one who wrote, "Kenya has one of the most liberal attitudes toward the press in Africa."[28] An employee in the ministry of information added:

> The government, just like anyone else, voices its disapproval on occasion when it feels that the press has distorted a government stand on a specific matter. Likewise, the government deplores attempts by the press to sensationalize relatively unimportant anti-government incidents. In every case, the press may defend its opinions.[29]

Only three nations—Botswana, Gambia, and Liberia—were perceived by informants as fitting into the social-libertarian philosophy. Minimal government controls are exerted to unclog channels of communication and assure operational spirit of the libertarian philosophy. In Africa, however, the definition is somewhat modified to place more emphasis on the relative freedom of the opposition political parties to get their views into the national press.

Such an interpretation of the social-libertarian concept limits the possible candidates to those with multiparty governments. In independent Africa, that means only 3 nations out of 34. The distinction, however, may be more technical than actual: Sir Seretse Khama's Botswana Democratic Party has ruled since independence (1966) and has 27 of 31 seats in parliament; in Gambia, Sir Danda Jawara's People's Progressive Alliance has ruled since independence (1965); and the True Whig Party of Liberia has been in power for the past half-century and the opposition party is practically nonexistent.

Informants in Gambia say there is a strong emphasis on the libertarian press philosophy and government does not interfere with the press. In Botswana and Liberia, however, there appear to be tendencies toward the social-centralist philosophy and attempts to harness the press for national development. A Botswana diplomat suggested national development is helped, not hindered, by the discussion of diverse viewpoints: "All the alternatives are screened and the best one is chosen in this way. "[30]

In conclusion, it must be emphasized that Table 7.2 is only a general classification of press philosophies in independent black Africa. Nations were classified primarily according to the perceived notions of local informants. Therefore, the table represents somewhat abstract perceptions rather than a rigorous definition of terms.

It should be remembered that the press philosophies are not mutually exclusive categories. All African nations exhibit characteristics of one or more press philosophies. The authoritarian concept and the social-centralist idea, in particular, overlap in many ways. For example, many African leaders rigidly control all aspects of the mass media and suppress public debate in the name of national development. Negative controls are exerted for positive goals.

It also has been noted that many African nations probably have no real concept of a press philosophy. Control and operation of the press are not the result of philosophic guidelines or enunciated policy but a reaction to daily problems of stability and survival. The reaction, however, is authoritarian in nature; most nations have grasped the potential of the press as an agent of development.

NOTES

1. E. Lloyd Sommerlad, "Problems in Developing a Free Enterprise Press in East Africa, " Gazette 14, no. 2 (1968); 77.

2. Fred S. Siebert, Theodore Peterson, and Wilbur Schramm, Four Theories of the Press (Urbana: University of Illinois Press, 1956).

3. John C. Merrill, "The Press and Social Responsibility," in International Communication, eds. Heinz-Dietrich Fischer and John C. Merrill (New York: Hastings House, 1970), p. 17.

4. William A. Hachten, Muffled Drums (Ames: Iowa State University Press, 1971), p. 44.

5. Ibid., p. 45.

6. Ibid., p. 272.

7. Ibid., p. 46.

8. John C. Merrill and Ralph L. Lowenstein, Media Messages and Men (New York: David McKay, 1971), p. 186.

9. Comment on mail questionnaire from Ghana, signed.

10. Comment on mail questionnaire from Botswana, signed.

11. Alhaji Babatunde Jose, "The Press in Nigeria," speech presented to the opening session of the Distripress in Athens, Greece, October 23, 1973, p. 4.

12. Letter from A. G. Fullerton, UNESCO Regional Information Office, Dakar, October 22, 1973.

13. Frank Barton, The Press in Africa (Nairobi: East African Publishing House, 1960), p. 39.

14. David O. Edeani, "Ownership and Control of the Press in Africa," Gazette 14, no. 2 (1970); 63.

15. Arnold Temu, University of Dar es Salaam, Tanzania, personal interview in April 1971.

16. Richard Hall, "The Press in Black Africa; How Free Is It?" Optima 18 (March 1968): 19.

17. Comment on mail questionnaire from Chad, anonymous.

18. Ghebeyehous Mekbib, first secretary at the embassy of Ethiopia, Washington, D. C., personal interview on January 10, 1974.

19. Comment on mail questionnaire regarding Ethiopia, signed.

20. Julius V. L. Soloku, information attaché at the embassy of Sierra Leone, Washington, D. C., personal interview on January 9, 1974.

21. William Koffi Adjoyi, counselor at the embassy of Togo, Washington, D. C., personal interview on January 9, 1974.

22. Comment on mail questionnaire from Zaïre, signed.

23. John M. Ostheimer, Nigerian Politics (New York: Harper and Row, 1973), p. 99.

24. Ildephonse Munyeshyaka, first secretary at the embassy of Rwanda, Washington, D. C., personal interview on January 11, 1974.

25. Hassan A. El Tayeb, counselor at the embassy of Sudan, Washington, D. C., personal interview on January 2, 1974.

26. Ferdinand E. Mwanza, first secretary at the embassy of Zambia, Washington, D. C., personal interview on January 9, 1974.

27. Voice of Uganda, Kampala, January 25, 1973.

28. Comment on mail questionnaire from Kenya, signed.
29. Comment on mail questionnaire from Kenya, signed.
30. Samuel A. Mpuchane, first secretary at the embassy of Botswana, Washington, D. C., personal interview on January 4, 1974.

8

COMPARING THE
AFRICAN MASS MEDIA

The extent of governmental press control in independent black Africa presents a melancholy picture to any individual who cherishes a belief in the free flow of information and the value of public debate.

Although a predominantly government-owned press can be excused in terms of the continent's present state of economic development, less justification can be found for the data indicating that over half of the 34 nations endorse an authoritarian press philosophy. Such an approach inhibits and stifles citizen participation in national decision making and development.

In other words, many African nations give lip service to the concept of positively harnessing the press for national development but precious little is being done in this direction. Comments from many African informants indicate that the problem is one of conceptualization. Rapid national development, in the minds of ruling elites, is expedited by the suppression of conflicting viewpoints and public debate. Unity is an important theme, on the assumption that a developing nation cannot afford the luxury of public debate that may fan the flames of "tribalism." Consequently, it is thought best for the mass media to present just one unified, official viewpoint.

The official viewpoint, in many cases, means the pronouncements of the ruling elites, who use the mass media to maintain the status quo and orchestrate unthinking public approval of government policies. In such a setting, little attempt is made to reach the masses with information that would improve their daily lives and perhaps arm them with enough knowledge to start questioning rank and privilege. Also inherent in the attitude of the ruling elites is the patronizing concept that only they know what is best for the nation—a thought pattern left over from the former colonial administrators.

The pervasiveness of government press control in independent black Africa is best illustrated by the following research findings:

1. The region has 71 daily newspapers; of this number, three-fourths (51) are owned by the government or the ruling political party.

2. Forty-five percent of the 34 nations presently have a wholly government-owned press in terms of all newspapers and magazines. No private or religious publications of general circulation exist.

3. Seventy percent of the governments own more than half of the nation's printing presses for newspapers and magazines. Of this number, 16 governments have over 75 percent ownership of the printing presses.

4. At least 15 nations have policies or legislation restricting foreign ownership of locally produced newspapers and magazines.

5. Seventy percent of the governments support newspapers and magazines through direct budgetary allocations or subsidies.

6. Almost 60 percent of the governments practice pre-publication censorship (this includes the 15 nations that have such review inherent in a wholly government-owned press).

7. Seventy percent of the governments exercise postpublication censorship of periodicals by banning, confiscation, or suspension.

8. Only three governments permit opposition political parties to publish newsletters or newspapers.

9. Nearly 45 percent of the governments have licensing and certification requirements for working journalists.

10. An independent judiciary free from political control is absent in 75 percent of the nations.

11. Half of the governments have a judiciary lacking power to review the constitutionality of legislation and edicts that may restrict the press.

12. Half the nations have preventive detention acts under which citizens and journalists can be held without charge or trial.

13. At least 85 percent of the nations have laws by which journalists can be fined or jailed for criticism or "disrespect" of government officials and policies.

14. Radio broadcasting is entirely government-owned and under the direct control of the head of government or the ministry of information. Governmental corporations are a rarity; autonomous public corporations are nonexistent.

15. Ninety percent of the nations have censorship boards or commissions that preview foreign entertainment films.

16. Sixty-five percent of the governments have banned or seized foreign periodicals in the past two years.

17. Seventy percent of the governments have exclusive contracts with international news agencies and process all foreign news before it is distributed to local media outlets.

There are few bright spots in the African press setting, but they are worth noting:

    1. Eighty-five percent of the nations with publications owned by both the government and private interests allocate newsprint without giving priority to government publications.

    2. Of the 19 nations that presently have a mixed government and private ownership of publications, at least 14 do not practice prepublication censorship.

    3. Nongovernmental newspapers and magazines generally are not required to post bond as a prerequisite for publishing.

    4. Of the 34 governments, 60 percent have broadcasting personnel employed under an ongoing civil service system.

    5. Over half the governments use professional training as a major criterion in appointing broadcast executives.

    6. Almost 70 percent of the governments do not formally censor outgoing cables of correspondents for foreign media.

The fundamental question arises, of course, as to how the black African nations compare with each other in terms of overall press controls. Does the Nigerian press, for example, actually have fewer governmental controls than the press in neighboring Ghana? The present literature makes that question difficult to answer because few studies have compared nations on a list of specific criteria that are applicable crossnationally.

The year-end press freedom reports of international news agencies like Associated Press (AP) and United Press International (UPI) make some effort to assess the free flow of information of a global basis, but such reports are not systematic and lack a common set of criteria. A nation usually is evaluated on the basis of incidents involving foreign newsmen, with little attention given to the problems of local journalists. Consequently, the judgments of AP and UPI correspondents usually are highly subjective and only a few nations are included in these annual reports. The Internaional Press Institute (IPI) also issues periodic reports on "incidents" in various nations, but there is no systematic comparison of countries.

PREVIOUS WORLD PRESS STUDIES

Perhaps the first person to utilize comparable and relatively stable categories for assessing the general level of press freedom (as defined in libertarian terms) around the world was Raymond Nixon. [1] He conducted one study in 1960, classifying 85 nations. Another study in 1963-64 was more refined and 117 nations were classified along the "free-controlled" continuum.

Nixon also used demographic data—gross national product, literacy, newspaper circulation per 1, 000 inhabitants—to support the hypothesis that there is a positive and systematic relationship between the degree of press freedom and the level of a country's general economic and educational development. Nixon wrote:

the higher the level of socio-economic development in a country, the greater likelihood that press freedom will exist; the lower the level of development, the greater the chance that press control will be found. [2]

Independent black Africa, of course, came off rather poorly in Nixon's study because it remains the least developed and poorest region in the world in terms of industrialization indexes. Of the 20 nations ranked by Nixon in his 1963-64 study (see Table 8.1), none even qualified for the first three levels of his nine-point scale ranging from a completely free press system to one wholly controlled. Most were in the intermediate (mixed) stages, exhibiting tendencies toward more or less control. Three nations (Ghana, Mali, and Upper Volta) fit the ninth level: a controlled press system—no qualifications.

Although Nixon utilized common categories for comparing the world's nations, his information is somewhat suspect because only five judges were used in his last study. Four of the judges (two from the United States and two from Europe) evaluated all 117 nations while a fifth judge was selected to render an opinion about a specific region or country. It is highly doubtful that these few people had the knowledge or background to adequately classify so many nations.

Nixon's studies were followed by a more comprehensive and quantitative project conducted by Ralph L. Lowenstein. [3] During 1966, he assayed the nations of the world in a Press Independence and Critical Ability (PICA) study to determine the relative levels of press freedom around the world. He used 23 specific criteria and asked informants in each country to assess the nations' level of press control under each criterion, utilizing a five-point verbal scale representing degrees of restraint. The scores of "native" and "non-native" judges were then used to rank nations on a seven-level free-controlled continuum.

Africa, however, was poorly represented in Lowenstein's world press survey. As in most international surveys, most of the returned questionnaires came from the relatively well developed nations. Mail questionnaires were sent to 25 nations in independent black Africa and 64 usable questionnaires were returned. Only 13 nations were eventually ranked because any nation with two or fewer returned questionnaires was eliminated from the study. Other black African nations were eliminated because countries with under million inhabitants were not included in the study.

TABLE 8.1

Press Controls in Black Africa
According to Nixon's 1965 Survey

System	Countries
Intermediate or mixed,with tendencies appearing to favor press system	Nigeria, Senegal, Sierra Leone, Uganda
Intermediate or mixed, with no clear tendencies toward either more freedom or more control	Congo, Ivory Coast, Kenya, Liberia, Tanzania, Togo, Zaïre
Intermediate or mixed, with tendencies appearing to favor controlled press system	Cameroon, Chad, Somalia, Sudan
Controlled, but with even less rigid controls and more opportunity for debate than next category	Ethiopia
Controlled, but with less rigid controls and some opportunity for debate	Guinea
Controlled—no qualifications	Ghana, Mali, Upper Volta

Note: The first three levels of Nixon's classification are not shown because they included no black African nations. The following nations were unranked in Nixon's survey: Botswana, Burundi, Central African Republic, Dahomey, Equatorial Guinea, Gabon, Gambia, Lesotho, Malawi, Mauritania, Niger, Rwanda, Swaziland, and Zambia.

According to Lowenstein's seven-level free-controlled continuum, none of the 13 ranked African nations met the criteria for the first two levels: free-high degree and free-moderate controls. Five nations were classified as free with many controls. Another three (Chad, Upper Volta, and Ethiopia) were ranked in the sixth level: controlled to a high degree. Table 8.2 also shows that Nigeria, Ghana, and Congo were in transition while Senegal and Cameroon were "controlled to a medium degree."

TABLE 8.2

Press Controls in Black Africa
According to Lowenstein's 1966 PICA Index

System	Countries
Free—high degree	None
Free—moderate controls	None
Free—many controls	Kenya, Malawi, Tanzania, Uganda, Zambia
Transitional	Congo, Ghana, Nigeria
Controlled—low degree	None
Controlled—medium degree	Cameroon, Senegal
Controlled—high degree	Chad, Ethiopia, Upper Volta

Note: The following countries were unranked: Botswana, Burundi, Central African Republic, Dahomey, Equatorial Guinea, Gabon, Gambia, Guinea, Ivory Coast, Lesotho, Liberia, Mali, Mauritania, Niger, Rwanda, Sierra Leone, Somalia, Sudan, Swaziland, Togo, Zaïre.

A NEW RANKING OF AFRICAN NATIONS

The research of Nixon and Lowenstein has contributed a great deal to measuring the relative degree of press freedom and controls around the world, but independent black Africa remains a somewhat unknown quantity.

Nixon utilized Americans and Europeans for his classification of 20 African nations; Lowenstein, although using both local and foreign judges, was able to classify less than 40 percent of the present 34 nations. In addition, both the Nixon and Lowenstein classification are now somewhat dated by the many changes in Africa during the last decade. There are several new nations, and the governments of other countries have been changed by military action or constitutional provisions recognizing formal one-party states.

This chaper therefore seeks to update the previous studies and offer a comprehensive overview of all 34 nations by devoting attention exclusively to assessing the nature of press-government relationships in contemporary black Africa. Previous chapters have explored in detail the types of specific press controls that exist in the African nations. It is now possible to organize the findings so that the overall level of press control in the various nations can be compared.

Unlike Nixon, who used the somewhat arbitrary evaluations of only five judges, this study has the advantage of enlisting a group of individuals for each country. No informant was asked to comment on

more than one nation, and the overwhelming majority of respondents
were African. In this way, over 200 individuals throughout the 34
nations and African embassy personnel in Washington, D. C., evaluated their own national press systems on 25 key criteria. These criteria are:

1. Newspaper ownership: Government ownership of all
daily newspapers in the country.
2. Printing ownership: Over 50 percent government ownership of the nation's printing presses for newspapers and magazines.
3. Budget allocation: Newspapers and magazines are
supported by direct governmental subsidies.
4. Newsprint allocation: Priority of government publications over private publications for allocation of newsprint
(includes nations with a wholly government-owned press).
5. Censorship: Prepublication review of newspapers
and magazines (inherent in a wholly government-owned press).
6. Suspension: Existence of government policy to ban,
suspend, seize, or confiscate newspapers and magazines.
7. Opposition publications: Publications of opposition
political parties are banned (includes formal one-party states
where only one party is constitutionally permitted).
8. Licensing journalists: Required governmental certification and licensing of working newsmen.
9. Licensing publications: Private newspapers and magazines must be registered or licensed by government (control
considered not applicable in nations with wholly government-
owned press).
10. Judicial appointment: Judiciary subject to dismissal
on political grounds.
11. Independent judiciary: Lack of judicial review concerning constitutionality of laws and regulations.
12. Preventive detention: Existence of preventive detention
acts to detain journalists and other citizens without charge or
trial.
13. Imprisonment: Fine or imprisonment for journalists who
imply "disrespect" or criticize the nation's leaders and policies.
14. Bond: Privately owned newspapers and magazines
must post bond to cover any potential libel or sedition damages
(control considered not applicable in nations with wholly government-owned press).
15. Libel laws: Nations with highly restrictive libel or
sedition laws as perceived by informants.
16. Broadcasting funds: National broadcasting is supported
through subsidy from general governmental funds or budgetary

allocations of a government ministry (as opposed to commercial advertising or license fees).

17. Broadcasting policy: Broadcasting adminstered by head of government, government minister, or ruling political party (as opposed to state-owned corporations and autonomous public corporations).

18. Broadcasting operations: Broadcasting facilities under daily supervision of officials of current government or ruling political party (as opposed to foreign technicians or trained local personnel).

19. Broadcasting personnel: Personnel employed in broadcasting are considered employees of current government or majority political party (as opposed to civil service, state corporation, or autonomous public corporation).

20. Broadcasting executives: Leadership in majority ruling party or past government service is major criterion for appointment of broadcasting executives (as opposed to civil service examinations or professional training).

21. Film censorship: Foreign entertainment films are screened by a government agency before being released for public viewing.

22. Foreign periodicals: Foreign periodicals were banned or confiscated by government in 1972-73.

23. Visa requirements: Special visa requirements are imposed by government on foreign journalists who wish to enter the country.

24. Cables: Foreign journalists are requested to submit cables for government approval before they are sent.

25. Foreign news agencies: Government has exclusive contractual agreements with international wire services.

Table 8.3 summarizes these 25 press controls on a crossnational basis. The table has utility in that readers can see at a glance what nations have what types of controls. However, the table should be used with the full knowledge that some data have been lost by summarizing. Informants in most nations expressed a low consensus on at least some press controls, and a scholar interested in greater analysis would be advised to review past chapters for detailed explanations of specific press controls.

However, the totals in Table 8.3 do provide a handy reference to what press controls are most pervasive in independent black Africa. An analysis of the 10 most pervasive controls (from totals column) is instructive in the respect that six are based on political considerations and not fiscal necessity, which has often been cited as an explanation by African leaders.

Thiry-one of the nations (90 percent of the total) prohibit or ban newspapers and magazines operated by opposition political groups.

TABLE 8.3

Summary of Press Controls by Country

Country	1	2	3	4	5	6	7	8	9	10	11	12	13	14	15	16	17	18	19	20	21	22	23	24	25
Botswana	x	x	x	x	x			x	x	x	*		x			x	x			x	x				
Burundi	x	x	x	x		x	x	x	x	x	x	*	x			x	x		x	x	x	x	*		x
Cameroon			x	x	x	x	x	x	x	x	*	x	x	n.a.		x	x		x	x	x	x			x
Central African Republic	x	x			x	x	x	*	n.a.	x	*	x	x			x	x			*	x	x	*		x
Chad	x	x	x	*	x	x	x	x	x	x	x	*	x	n.a.		x	x		x	x	x	x	x	x	x
Congo	x	x	x	x	x	x	x	x	n.a.	x	x	x	x	n.a.		x	x		x	x	x	x	x		x
Dahomey	x	x	x	x	x	x	x	x	x	x	x	*	x			x	x			x	x	x		x	x
Equatorial Guinea	n.a.	x	x		x	x	x	x	n.a.	x		x	x	n.a.		x	x		x	x	x	x	x	x	x
Ethiopia	x	x	x	x	x	x	x	x	x	x	x	x	x	n.a.		x	x		x	x	x	x	x		x
Gabon	x	x	x	x	x	x	x	x	n.a.	x			x	n.a.	x	x	x			x	x	x			x
Gambia	n.a.	x				x	x	x	x	x	*		x	x		x	x				x				
Ghana	x	x	x		x	x	x	x	x	x	x	x	x			x	x				x				x
Guinea	x	x	x	x	x		x	x	n.a.	x	x	*	n.a.	n.a.		x	x		x	x	x	x	x	x	x
Ivory Coast	x	x	x	x	x	x	x	*	n.a.	x	x	x	*	n.a.		x	x			x	x	x		x	x
Kenya	x	x				x	x	x	x	x		x	x	x		x	x					x			
Lesotho	x	x	x		x	x	x	x	x	*	x	x	x			x	x				x				x
Liberia	x	x	x		x	x	x	x	x	x	x	x	x		x		x				x	x	x	*	*
Malawi	x	x	x	x	x	x	x	*	n.a.	x	x	x	x	n.a.		x	x			*	x	x	x		x
Mali	x	x	x	x	x	x	x	x	n.a.	x	x	x	*	n.a.	x	x	x				x	x	x		x
Mauritania	x	x	x	x	x		x		n.a.				x	n.a.	x	x	x			*	x		x		x
Niger	x	x	x		x	*	x	*	n.a.	x	*		x	n.a.			x		x		x	*			x
Nigeria	n.a.	x	x				x			x		x				x	x		x		x	x			
Rwanda	x	x	x		x	x	x		x	x	x		x			x	x				x				x
Senegal	x	x	x	x	x	x	x	x	n.a.		x	x	*	n.a.		x	x				x	x			
Sierra Leone	x	x	x	x	x	x	x	x	x	x	x	x	*			x	x		x	*	x	x	x		x
Somalia	x	x		x	x	x	x	x	n.a.	x	x	x	x	n.a.	x	x	x				x	x		*	x
Sudan	x	x		x	x	x	x	x	n.a.	x		x	x	n.a.		x	x		x	x	x	x			x
Swaziland	n.a.	x	x		x	x	x	x	x	x	x	x	x			x	x		x	x	x	x			
Tanzania	x	x			x	x	x	x	x	x	x	x	x			x	x				x				
Togo	x	x	x	x	x	x	x	x	n.a.	x	x	x	x	n.a.		x	x		x	x	x	x	x		x
Uganda	x	x			x	x	x	x	x	x	x	*	x		x	x	x				x	x			
Upper Volta			x	x	x	x	x	x	x	x	*	x	x			x	x		x	*	x		x	*	
Zaïre	x	x	x		x	x	x	x	n.a.	x	x	x	x	n.a.	x	x	x		x	x	x	x	x		x
Zambia		x	x		x	x	x	x	x	x	*	x	x			x	x				x	x	*		x
Total	20	25	24	16	20	24	31	17	18	26	18	18	29	2	8	32	31	0	10	12	31	22	8	3	23

* Insufficient information.
Note: See text for explanation of controls.

An equal number routinely engage in film censorship. Eighty-five percent (29) also tend to control individual journalists by fine or imprisonment when officials feel they have been critical of government policies.

Another major political control is the operation of broadcasting services directly under the head of government or a minister of government in 90 percent of the nations. In such cases, there is no buffer zone provided by state-owned corporations or autonomous public corporations with separate boards of directors. Over two-thirds of the governments also exercise the power to ban or seize publications considered politically sensitive. The courts cannot protect publications from arbitrary control because the concept of an independent judiciary is not present in 26 of the nations; the general pattern is for the courts to be fused with the executive branch.

The most prevalent fiscal control is exerted over broadcasting services. Commercial advertising and license fees provide such a small percentage of the needed funds that current governments must provide large sums of money. This is the case in 95 percent of the nations, and the financial dependence on government makes broadcasting particularly sensitive to the whims of the bureaucrats in power.

Another fiscal control is the government ownership and operation of printing presses. Almost three-fourths of the governments own more than 50 percent of the printing presses in their nations, primarily because there is a lack of private capital to build printing plants. It remains an awesome power, however, because only officially sanctioned publications can get published. Another 24 nations exert fiscal control over the newspapers and magazines by financing them with government allocations or subsidies. And, finally, exclusive governmental contracts with international news agencies (23 nations) often are based on economics, but the result is the official filtering of all foreign news.

Table 8.3 also shows the number of press controls exerted in each nation. This number is derived by counting the number of affirmative responses to the 25 listed controls. Conceivably, a nation could have a score of up to 25 if informants gave affirmative answers on all 25 criteria and their answers were substantiated by supplemental research.

On this basis, then, one can easily rank the 34 nations on a continuum from minimal to total control. Table 8.4 provides this ranking by number of controls, but it should be pointed out that a somewhat different profile might emerge if one could adequately weight the specific controls in terms of relative importance. Whether a nation exercises prepublication censorship, for example, is probably more important in terms of overall control than whether foreign entertainment films are censored on grounds of morality and political content.

In several nations, there is insufficient information about the existence of specific controls. There is insufficient information, for example, to record Niger and Malawi on four controls. The response rate from both nations was relatively poor and additional research could not document these controls. Niger, however, has been placed under more rigid control since a military coup in April 1974 overthrew President Hamani Diori, who had ruled since independence in 1960. Malawi, based on the reported actions of President Banda, would undoubtedly have a higher number of controls, but documented information is scarce.

Nixon used nine classifications and Lowenstein found seven to be most useful. For purposes of this ranking, it seems that five levels of press control are the most meaningful. Table 8.5 is based on classification of groups by five controls. From 0 to 5 controls, for example, can be described as minimal control. Nations with 6 to 10 controls are described as having low control, while countries with 11 to 15 controls have medium control. A nation classified as having high control would have 16 to 20 controls, and those with 21 to 25 controls would be considered under total control.

By using such a classification scheme, about three-fourths of the governments in independent black Africa can be described as exerting medium or high control on their mass media systems. Another 23 percent (eight nations) exercise low control; only one nation, Liberia, barely fits the classification of minimal control with five controls. No nation in black Africa is in the category of total control, but Congo and Guinea approach it with 20 controls each.

COMPARISON WITH PREVIOUS STUDIES

It is worth comparing the current data with the rankings of Nixon and Lowenstein in their earlier studies. Such a comparison, to a certain degree, indicates the changes in some countries. Table 8.5 is prepared for this purpose. Nixon, for example, noted that four nations—Nigeria, Senegal, Sierra Leone, and Uganda—had mixed systems that appeared to favor a free press concept. Present data seem to indicate that these nations, especially Nigeria and Senegal, retain their tendency toward a free press, having a low number of controls. Sierra Leone and Uganda, however, are ranked in Table 8.4 as having a medium number of controls, and the tendency seems to be toward a more controlled press.

Perhaps the most striking change since Nixon's 1965 study involves his classification of nations with no clear tendency toward either more freedom or more press control. Nixon listed seven nations in this category: Congo, Zaïre, Ivory Coast, Kenya, Liberia, Tanzania, and Togo. Today, the research shows that three of those nations—Congo, Zaïre, and Togo—now rank among the nations with high levels of control. The Congo and Zaïre have moved to a highly centralized one-party concept while Togo is under military control.

TABLE 8.4

Ranking of Black African Nations
by Number of Press Controls

		Number of Countries	Percentage of Total
Minimal control (0-5)		1	2.94
Liberia (5)			
Low control (6-10)		8	23.53
Gambia (8)	Botswana (10)		
Zambia (8)	Ghana (10)		
Kenya (9)	Nigeria (10)		
Rwanda (9)	Senegal (10)		
Medium control (11-15)		12	35.29
Niger (11)	Uganda (13)		
Tanzania (11)	Cameroon (14)		
Lesotho (12)	Mauritania (14)		
Swaziland (12)	Upper Volta (14)		
Ivory Coast (13)	Malawi (15)		
Sierra Leone (13)	Sudan (15)		
High control (16-20)		13	38.24
Chad (16)	Equatorial Guinea (18)		
Dahomey (16)	Ethiopia (18)		
Burundi (17)	Togo (18)		
Central African	Somalia (19)		
Republic (17)	Zaïre (19)		
Gabon (17)	Congo (20)		
Mali (17)	Guinea (20)		
Total control (21-25)		0	0
Total		34	100

TABLE 8.5

Comparison of Press Surveys

Country	Nixon Ranking (1965)	Lowenstein Ranking (1966)	Current Ranking (1974)
Botswana	–	–	low control
Burundi	–	–	high control
Cameroon	mixed system toward control		medium control
Central African Republic		controlled–medium degree	high control
Chad	mixed system toward control	controlled–high degree	high control
Congo	mixed system–no trend	transitional	high control
Dahomey	–		high control
Equatorial Guinea			high control
Ethiopia	controlled–medium degree	controlled–high degree	high control
Gabon	–		high control
Gambia			low control
Ghana	controlled–no qualifications	transitional	low control
Guinea	controlled–medium degree		high control
Ivory Coast	mixed system–no trend		medium control
Kenya	mixed system–no trend	free–many controls	low control
Lesotho	–		medium control
Liberia	mixed systems–no trend		minimal control
Malawi	controlled–no qualifications	free–many controls	medium control
Mali	–		high control
Mauritania			medium control
Niger			medium control
Nigeria	mixed system toward freedom	transitional	low control
Rwanda	–		low control
Senegal	mixed system toward freedom	controlled–medium degree	medium control
Sierra Leone	mixed system toward freedom		high control
Somalia	mixed system toward control		medium control
Sudan	mixed system toward control		medium control
Swaziland			medium control
Tanzania	mixed system–no trend	free–many controls	medium control
Togo	mixed system–no trend		high control
Uganda	mixed system toward freedom	free–many controls	medium control
Upper Volta	controlled–no qualifications	controlled–high degree	medium control
Zaïre	mixed system–no trend		high control
Zambia	–	free–many controls	low control

128

Liberia shows the greatest change, currently being ranked as the only nation in the category of minimal controls. One explanation involves the liberalization policies of President William Tolbert, who took office in 1971 after the death of William Tubman. The former president was known as a highly autocratic leader; during his many years of tenure, few civil liberties were observed in Liberia. Tolbert, on the other hand, has introduced an atmosphere of public debate, and citizens are now speaking out again on various issues. Some informants in Liberia, taking a dimmer view, say the country ranks low on formal controls but there are still a number of unwritten restraints and all journalists exercise self-censorship. In addition, the legislature passed an expanded sedition law in March 1974, and many journalists feel that this may mean increased restraints on the press.

Nixon ranked four nations as having definite tendencies toward controlled press systems: Cameroon, Chad, Somalia, and Sudan. The current data seem to support this, although Cameroon and Sudan have fewer tendencies in this direction than the other two nations. Sudan, for example, has a nationalized press but also has two rival publishing houses.

Ethiopia remains in the same comparative position, with little change in the pattern of numerous press controls. The recent takeover by the military and the fall of Haile Selassie from power probably will not change the pattern much in the near future but might mean more opportunity for public debate if the military implements its stated plans for a one-party system based on socialist principles. Guinea also retains its highly structured press philosophy, and there has been little change since Nixon's 1965 study; if anything, the tendency has been for more control

Nixon classified three nations as completely controlled press systems: Ghana, Mali, and Upper Volta. In 1974, it appeared that the classification was no longer valid. Ghana, for example, is no longer under Nkrumah's highly centralized "revolutionary" press concept; the current military regime has allowed the press more freedom. Government newspapers and broadcasting facilities are under the auspices of a government corporation, and privately owned newspapers are allowed to publish. Mali is under a military government, but the regime has indicated a willingness to return the country to civilian rule. In Upper Volta, the military regime has been extremely progressive and is credited by most observers with saving the nation from utter chaos. General (and now president) Sangoule Lamizana, from all indications, is directing his energies to reestablishing a multiparty government even though there have been setbacks.

Although the categories are not exactly comparable, Lowenstein's 1966 PICA study provides some general comparisons. For example, he ranked five nations as free with many controls: Kenya, Zambia, Tanzania, Uganda, and Malawi. Present data indicate that Kenya and

Zambia have a low number of controls. The other three nations have a
medium number of controls, with Malawi having the most (15). This
is probably the result of the nation becoming a highly centralized
one-party state under President Banda, who has expressed his disdain
for the press on a number of occasions. Uganda also has shifted toward
more control under the regime of General Amin, who seized power in
1971. It is ironic that one of the reasons given by Amin for taking power
was the lack of free speech in the country under President Milton Obote.

Nigeria, Ghana, and Congo were listed as transitional states by
Lowenstein in 1966. Current research shows that Ghana and Nigeria,
despite military regimes, have tended toward fewer government controls
while the Congo now has almost total control of the press. A people's
republic along Marxist-Leninist lines was declared in 1969. Senegal
and Cameroon still occupy the middle range of government controls,
with Senegal having significantly fewer controls than Cameroon.

Lowenstein ranked Chad, Upper Volta, and Ethiopia as controlled
to a high degree. Current information shows that Upper Volta has
moved toward fewer controls—a private daily was started in 1973 and
opposition parties were permitted until February 1974. Chad and
Ethiopia still have a high number of controls. Their relative position
is only ameliorated by the fact that other nations exhibit even more
government control.

In terms of surveys on political freedom, the majority of the nations
in the first two categories in Table 8.4 also were listed as partly free
or free by Freedom House of New York in a 1973 annual world survey. [4]
Gambia, however, was the only nation in black Africa considered free
by Freedom House, which based its ranking on selected political
indexes.

POSSIBLE VARIABLES IN PREDICTING DEGREE OF PRESS CONTROL

The survey of political freedom by Freedom House, and the research
of Nixon and Lowenstein, generally support the thesis that the nations
with the fewest press controls and the most press freedom are those
with some form of democratic government. Africa's three multiparty
states—Botswana, Gambia, and Liberia—are listed in Table 8.4 among
the nations with the fewest formalized press restraints.

Yet caution should be exercised in taking the general concept at
face value, especially in independent black Africa. Zambia also is
listed as having low press controls, and it is a formal one-party state.
Kenya is a de facto one-party state, but most observers feel it has one
of the freest press systems in black Africa.

The current research also contradicts the general assumption that
military regimes automatically mean a highly restricted press system.

Ghana, Nigeria, and Rwanda are under military control but, on a comparative basis, they have low press control. The military states of Togo and Somalia, on the other hand, more accurately fit the stereotype by having highly controlled press systems. Obviously, there are differences in types of military governments, based on each nation's cultural and political traditions.

Monarchies also are difficult to pigeonhole. Swaziland under King Sobhuza II has far fewer press restraints than Ethiopia had under Emperor Haile Selassie. Perhaps one explanation is the evolution of the two nations. Swaziland's monarch was subject to British administration prior to independence in 1968. At that time, the new constitution provided for a parliamentary form of government. Ethiopia's revised constitution, however, merely reaffirmed the emperor's traditional powers.

African nations in the middle ranges of press control (see Table 8.5) exhibit several forms of government. There are military regimes, de facto one-party states, and formal one-party states. About the only generalization that can be made is by comparing the extreme categories. Multiparty governments, as already noted, tend to have a lower number of controls while highly centralized military regimes and constitutionally recognized one-party states have high controls. As previously noted, however, there are exceptions.

Togo and Somalia represent the military regimes in Africa with the greatest number of press controls. Equatorial Guinea, Zaïre, Congo, and Guinea are the formal one-party states with the greatest number of controls. All four share the characteristic of having a strong, powerful leader; Macia Nguema of Equatorial Guinea, for example, is president for life. Some political scientists also have noted that these nations have one-party systems based on small ruling elites rather than mass participation, as is found in Tanzania.

An analysis of ownership patterns perhaps is more predictive of level of government press controls. In general, nations with a mixed ownership system—publications owned by both government and private interests—have the fewest formal press controls and restraints. The nine nations in the first two categories of Table 8.5, for example, all have mixed ownership of print media. Botswana is included since until recently it had two private weeklies, which have suspended publication due to financial reasons. South African newspapers, however, circulate freely in the country.

The 12 nations with medium controls are about evenly divided, with a mixed ownership system having the slight edge. However, the number of nations with a wholly government-owned press continues to increase in the next category of high control, with almost 80 percent of such nations having a wholly government-owned press.

Several factors in addition to form of government and ownership patterns also were analyzed in terms of predicting level of press controls: (1) length of independence, (2) colonial heritage, and (3) stability of present government.

One hypothesis advanced is that an older nation will have fewer press controls because the country has had the time to stabilize and find its identity. Liberia, founded in 1847 and the only nation with minimal controls, provides some support of the hypothesis, but other categories offer few supporting data. The three oldest nations in black Africa in terms of independence from colonial rule are scattered throughout the remaining categories. Ghana (1957) has low controls but Sudan (1956) is at the far end of the medium control range. Guinea (1958) has the highest number of controls in independent black Africa. But Gambia and Botswana, which achieved independence in 1965, are among the nations with the lowest number of press controls.

The date of independence probably has less to do with relative press freedom than the colonial legacy and the models inherited by African leaders. It already has been documented that many colonial institutions, particularly legal codes and administrative techniques, were adopted by the newly independent African nations because of the lack of indigenous institutions that could cope with the modern world in terms of international finance, widespread public services, and governing millions of people in a nation-state.

African leaders also inherited press institutions and a whole set of legal restraints from former colonial rulers. Historical research indicates that the press in French Africa was particularly suppressed and few indigenous publications ever saw the light of day.

The French believed in direct rule from France and one objective of domination was to replace African culture with "civilized" French institutions and values. Education and literacy, however, were highly selective processes and only a few Africans ever became model "Frenchmen." At least 90 percent of the African people under French rule never became literate or were taught about civil liberties. A local press never had the opportunity for development and even today there is a lack of press tradition in many Francophone nations. This also was true in the Belgian and Spanish colonies.

The British, on the other hand, had no intention of making the African peoples into Englishmen. Colonial policy was based on the concept of indirect rule and there was a conscious effort to harness local institutions for local administration. The English, for example, codified tribal law in East Africa and even created written alphabets for major African languages. Chiefs often retained their power on the local level (the Buganda of Uganda is a good example), and more Africans became literate under the British missionary influence. In brief, the British form of administration created a situation where indigenous newspapers were permitted—if not exactly welcomed—and could become spokesmen for African feelings about independence.

The tradition of the press, consequently, is much different in Francophone and Anglophone Africa. The colonial heritage is still evident today in an analysis of relative press controls.

Three-fourths of the nations with low controls (see Table 8.5), for example, have a British colonial background. Senegal and Rwanda are the only exceptions. Anglophone nations also dominate the next category of medium controls; eight of these nations had such a background. There are no Anglophone nations in the category of high controls; most of these countries have a French background but two—Burundi and Zaïre—were Belgian. Somalia has an essentially Italian background, while Equatorial Guinea was ruled by Spain.

Liberia, of course, has no colonial background since it was established by freed slaves from the United States. They became the ruling elite over the indigenous peoples and modeled the nation's constitution on that of the United States. The freed slaves also set up an essentially American-British legal code and adopted the American view of press freedom, although it was not always practiced.

This heritage probably explains why Liberia is ranked so high in comparison to other African nations. But the country has been continually overlooked by the current literature because it is not exactly the crossroads of Africa. In addition, more populous Nigeria and more readily accessible Kenya have been given greater attention in one-country studies. Both nations also have larger and more developed press systems.

The relative stability of governments appears to have some correlation with the presence of press control. Seven of the nine nations in the minimal and low classifications (see Table 8.5) have had the same government for a number of years. Liberia does not deviate from this pattern since there has been a continuity of government under William Tolbert, who previously served as vice president. Five nations—Gambia, Zambia, Kenya, Botswana, and Senegal—have had the same government since independence. Nigeria's current regime was instituted in 1966. Only Ghana and Rwanda have had a major change of government since 1969, due to military takeovers.

However, the proportion of nations with major changes of government since 1969 increases in the next categories of medium and high control. Both classifications list four nations that have had major political upheavals in the past five years. Niger should be added to this list because a military coup occurred in April 1974. The bulk of this study, however, had been completed prior to that time.

The five variables discussed above give some preliminary insight into the types of nations with high or low press controls. The analysis provides a somewhat composite profile of the African nation with low controls: It would be a country with a British colonial background and mixed government-private ownership of media facilities, multiparty government, and no major political upheaval for five or more years.

HOPE FOR THE FUTURE?

The colonial legacy has strongly shaped the contemporary African press, although few Africans will admit this. They would prefer to forget the unpleasantness of colonial domination, but it is an exercise in self-deception since most national press systems are still modeled on the attitudes and strictures of colonial administrators. France, Belgium, Spain, Italy, and England (perhaps to a lesser extent) introduced a somewhat authoritarian press philosophy and suppressed the development of an indigenous press.

The second major influence in the development of the African press involved the polemics of nationalism. Aspiring African leaders first harnessed the press for the purpose of inspiring the masses and rallying support for political causes. Factual reporting and use of the press as a forum for divergent ideas have yet to develop in many African nations. These concepts probably will not take hold until the present heads of government, who used the press in the fight for independence, are replaced by a second generation of new leaders who can perceive the role of the press in different ways.

It is doubtful that the present profile of press ownership and restraints in independent black Africa will change in the near future. Most nations are still finding some sense of nationhood and lack the self-confidence to permit a robust discussion of public issues. The lack of capital also remains a serious problem, and government will remain the only institution in most nations that is large enough to amass the kind of capital necessary to operate press systems.

In fact, it may well be that black Africa will never have the type of press systems found in the West. The libertarian press concept is partly based on the idea of a multiparty government, and Africa shows little inclination to develop in that direction. By the same token, it is highly unlikely that most African nations will opt for the communist system of press operation. The most likely pattern probably will involve constitutionally recognized one-party states but a degree of pluralism in press ownership. Political conflict may be absent from newspaper pages, but citizens will be able to read information on a variety of topics that would be considered a waste of space in Soviet newspapers because such articles do little or nothing to advance ideology. African nations are less concerned about ideology and more concerned about the pressures of daily survival.

There is room for optimism. Africa's vast resources are now being tapped and multiple programs of national development will slowly raise the standard of living for all Africans. Industrialization and urbanization are making millions of African wage earners, for better or worse, and they are beginning to have disposable incomes.

More than one statistical analysis has shown that consumption of
newspapers, radio, and television rises directly with gross national
product per capita. [5] Such a pattern would indicate that black Africa
will have more pluralistic press systems in the future—that is, a healthy
mix of government and privately owned publications that will serve
large audiences. It has already been shown that nations with mixed
ownership generally have fewer controls.

The pattern of African nations also shows that rising income levels
are related to freer press systems. The nine nations in the first two
categories of press controls (see Table 8. 5) have an average per capita
income of $179 annually. The 12 nations listed as having medium
control have GNP of $151, while GNP in nations with high control
falls to $120 per capita. [6]

Rising income and literacy levels in Africa means that the continent
will pass through a period of the "penny" press like that which served
the new literates of the United States during the nineteenth-century.
Many nations already have newspapers tabloids, comic books, and
racy magazines that cater to the lowest common denominator by offering
murder, sex, and scandal. Lagos Week-End is extremely popular in
Nigeria, and Flamingo finds thousands of readers in Uganda. Nigerian
levels of disposable income and literacy have advanced to the stage
that a new magazine, New Breed, is making a profit by catering to the
growing middle class. The age of the mass popular press is now
dawning in black Africa.

Hopefully, penny press will develop the people's appetite for more
serious news and a growing army of literates will demand a freer flow
of information. An educated public will no longer be content to have
information censored or restricted by a small, patronizing elite. But
only time will tell whether this optimism is justified.

NOTES

1. Raymond Nixon, "Freedom in the World's Press: A Fresh Appraisal with New Data, " Journalism Quarterly 52 (Winter 1965): 3-14, 118-
19. Also see "Factors Related to Freedom in National Press Systems, "
in International Communication, eds. Heinz-Dietrich Fischer and John
C. Merrill (New York: Hastings House, 1970), pp. 115-28.

2. Nixon, "Freedom in the World's Press, " p. 7.

3. Ralph L. Lowenstein, "Measuring World Press Freedom as a
Political Indicator, " Ph. D. dissertation, University of Missouri, 1967.
Also see "Press Freedom as a Political Indicator, " in International
Communication, eds. Fischer and Merrill, pp. 129-40.

4. "The Comparative Survey of Freedom, " Freedom at Issue
(Freedom House), January-February 1973, p. 4.

5. Dennis L. Wilcox and Keith P. Sanders, "A Multi-State Model of Global Media Progression," unpublished research paper, 1974. A statistical correlation of demographic variables in 33 nations showed that mass media consumption correlated with income at the following levels: television, 0.91; radio receivers, 0.85; newspapers, 0.81.

6. Gabon is excluded from this averaging because it skews the general pattern. It is one of the least populated (500,000) nations in Africa, but its vast reserves of manganese, iron ore, and uranium give it the highest per capita income ($630) in black Africa. Yet the country is even less developed on other socioeconomic indexes than its more populous neighbors. It is a situation not unlike that in phosphate-rich Nauru in the South Pacific, which has a per capita income of $4,000 although the island has no television, a small radio station, and only a weekly mimeographed bulletin.

TABLE A. 1

Number of Daily Newspapers in Continental Africa
As Compared with Other World Areas

Number of Dailies	1969	Copies Per 1,000
World	7,680	130
Africa	210	19
North America	1,880	295
Latin America	1,085	61
East Asia	360	341
South Asia	1,600	16
Europe	1,800	259
Oceania	114	296
USSR	630	321

Note: East Asia figures include People's Republic of China, Hong Kong, Mongolia, Macao, Japan, Republic of Korea, North Korea, and Ryukyu Islands. South Asia includes the rest of Asia.
Source: UNESCO Statistical Yearbook (Paris: UNESCO, 1972), p. 751.

TABLE A. 2

Number of Radio Receivers in Continental Africa
As Compared with Other World Areas

| Area | 1969 Figures | |
	Radio Receivers (millions)	Sets Per 1, 000 Population
World	653	232
Africa	15. 6	45
North America	300	1, 339
Latin America	46	167
East Asia	32	192
South Asia	36	33
Europe	129	280
Oceania	3. 6	190
USSR	90. 1	375

Note: East Asia figures include People's Republic of China, Hong
Kong, Mongolia, Macao, Japan, Republic of Korea, North Korea, and
Ryukyu Islands. South Asia includes rest of Asia.
Source: UNESCO Statistical Yearbook (Paris: UNESCO, 1972), p.
806.

TABLE A. 3

Number of Television Receivers in Continental Africa
As Compared with Other World Areas

| Area | 1 969 Figures | |
	Television Receivers (millions)	Sets Per 1, 000 Population
World	251	89
Africa	1. 1	3. 2
North America	89	397
Latin America	15	54
East Asia	23	1 38
South Asia	2. 5	2. 3
Europe	86. 5	188
Oceania	3. 3	175
USSR	30. 7	128

Note: East Asia figures include People's Republic of China, Hong
Kong, Mongolia, Macao, Japan, Republic of Korea, North Korea, and
Ryukyu Islands. South Asia includes rest of Asia.
Source: UNESCO Statistical Yearbook (Paris: UNESCO, 1972),
p. 837.

TABLE A. 4

Scarcity of Mass Media Facilities in Independent Black Africa

Country	Daily Newspapers Per 1,000	Radio Receivers Per 1,000	TV Receivers Per 1,000
Botswana	n. a.	13	no system
Burundi	n. a.	18	no system
Cameroon	2	n. a.	no system
Central African Republic	0. 6	30	no system
Chad	0. 4	16	no system
Congo (Brazzaville)	1. 3	69	1. 9
Dahomey	0. 4	32	no system
Equatorial Guinea	4	n. a.	n. a.
Ethiopia	2	6	0. 3
Gabon	n. a.	124	n. a.
Gambia	n. a.	137	no system
Ghana	34	78	1. 8
Guinea	n. a.	23	no system
Ivory Coast	3	17	2. 4
Kenya	13	48	1. 5
Lesotho	n. a.	5	no system
Liberia	n. a.	132	6
Malawi	n. a.	20	no system
Mali	0. 4	12	no system
Mauritania	n. a.	47	no system
Niger	0. 4	25	n. a.
Nigeria	7	23	1. 4
Rwanda	n. a.	8	no system
Senegal	5	69	0. 4
Sierra Leone	10	56	1. 4
Somalia	2	18	no system
Sudan	14	n. a.	2. 2
Swaziland	n. a.	32	no system
Tanzania	3	11	0. 3
Togo	7	22	no system
Uganda	8	n. a.	1. 3
Upper Volta	0. 4	16	n. a.
Zaïre	1	4	0. 4
Zambia	15	18	5

Source: UNESCO Statistical Yearbook (Paris: UNESCO, 1972), p. 751; "World Nations" in The Official Associated Press Yearbook for 1973 (New York: Almanac, 1972), pp. 631-797.

APPENDIX B

BOTSWANA
Daily News
(Government)
Information Services
Gaborone

BURUNDI
Flash Infor
(Government)
Ministry of Information
Box 1400
Bujumbura

CAMEROON
L'Agence Camerounaise de Presse
(ACAP) Bulletin
(Government)
B. P. 1170
Yaoundé
La Presse du Cameroun[1]
(Private)
B. P. 584
Douala

CENTRAL AFRICAN REPUBLIC
Bangui La So (Bulletin)
(Government)
Centrafic-Press News Agency
B. P. 1290
Bangui

CHAD
Info-Tchad (Bulletin)
(Government)
Agence Tchadienne de Presse (ATP)
B. P. 670
N'Djamena (Fort-Lamy)

CONGO
Bulletin Quotidien de l'Information[2]
(Government)
B. P. 2144
Brazzaville

DAHOMEY
Daho-Express
(Government)
B. P. 1210
Cotonou

EQUATORIAL GUINEA
No daily newspaper or bulletin

ETHIOPIA
Addis Soir
(Government)
Addis Ababa
Addis Zemen
(Government)
P. O. Box 222
Addis Ababa
Hebret
(Government)
Asmara
Il Giornale dell' Eritera
(Government)
Asmara
Il Quotidiano Eritera
(Private)
Asmara

GABON
Gabon Matin (Bulletin)
(Government)
B. P. 168
Libreville

GAMBIA
No daily newspaper or bulletin

GHANA
Daily Graphic

(Government corporation)
Brewery Road
P. O. Box 742
Accra
Ghanaian Times
(Government Corporation)
P. O. Box 2638
Accra
The Pioneer
(Private)
P. O. Box 325
Kumasi

GUINEA
Horoya
(Ruling party)
B. P. 141
Conakry

IVORY COAST
Bulletin Quotidien
(Government)
Agence Ivoirienne de Presse (AIP)
B. P. 4312
Abidjan
Fraternité-Matin
(Government)
B. P. 1807
Abidjan

KENYA
Daily Nation
(Private)
P. O. Box 49010
Nairobi
East African Standard
(Private)
P. O. Box 30080
Nairobi
Evening News [3]
(Private)
Nairobi
Taifa Leo
(Private)
P. O. Box 49010
Nairobi

LESOTHO
Koena News Bulletin
(Government)
Department of Information
P. O. Box 353
Maseru

LIBERIA
Liberian Star
(Government corporation)
P. O. Box 691
Monrovia

MALAWI
Daily Times [4]
(Private)
P. O. Box 458
Blantyre

MALI
L'Essor
(Government)
B. P. 470
Bamako

MAURITANIA
Office de Nouakchott-Information
   (Bulletin)
(Government)
Presse Ecrite et des Relations
   Exteriéures
B. P. 371
Nouakchott

NIGER
Le Temps du Niger
(Government)
B. P. 368
Niamey

NIGERIA [5]
Daily Express
(Private)
5-11 Apongbon Street
Lagos
Daily Sketch

(Government of Western State)
New Court Road
P. M. B. 5067
Ibadan
Daily Times
(Private)
3, 5, 7 Kakawa Street
Lagos
Evening Times
(Private)
3, 5, 7 Kakawa Street
Lagos
Irchin
(Private)
16 Bambgose Street
Lagos
Morning Post[6]
(Federal government)
2 Malu Road
Lagos
New Nigerian
(Government of North-Central State)
11 Dawaki Road
Kaduna
Nigerian Chronicle[7]
(Private)
P. M. B. 1074
Calabar
Nigerian Herald
(Government of Kwara State)
Jebba
Nigerian Observer
(Government of Mid-Western State)
18 Airport Road
Benin City
Nigerian Standard[8]
(Government of Benue Plateau State)
5, Zaïre By-Pass
Jos
Nigerian Tribune
(Private)
P. O. Box 78
Ibadan
Renaissance
(Government of East Central State)
9 Works Road
Enugu

West African Pilot
(Private)
34 Commercial Avenue
Yaba

RWANDA
No daily newspaper or bulletin

SENEGAL
Le Soleil
(Government corporation)
B. P. 92
Dakar

SIERRA LEONE
Daily Mail
(Government)
29, Rawdon Street
Freetown
Freedom
(Government)
Freetown
The Nation
(Government)
Water Street
Freetown

SOMALIA
Najmat Oktober
(Government)
Ministry of Information and
   National Guidance
Mogadiscio
Xiddigta Oktobar
(Government)
Ministry of Information and
   National Guidance
Mogadiscio

SUDAN
Al Sahafa
(Ruling political party)
P. O. Box 1228
Khartoum
El Rai El Amm
(Ruling political party)
P. O. Box 424

Khartoum
Sudan Mirror
(Ruling political party)
Khartoum

SWAZILAND
No daily newspaper or bulletin

TANZANIA[9]
Daily News
(Government corporation)
P. O. Box 9033
Dar es Salaam
Ngurumo
(Private)
P. O. Box 937
Dar es Salaam
Uhuru
(Ruling political party)
P. O. Box 9221
Dar es Salaam

TOGO
Togo Presse
(Government)
B. P. 891
Lome

UGANDA
Munno[10]
(Private)
P. O. Box 4027
Kampala
Omukulembeze
(Government)
P. O. Box 7041
Kampala
Taifa Empya
(Private)
P. O. Box 1986
Kampala
Voice of Uganda[11]
(Government)

Ministry of Information
Kampala

UPPER VOLTA
Bulletin Quotidien d' Information
(Government)
Bobo-Dioulasso
Carrefour Africain
B. P. 368
Ouagadougou
L'Observateur
(Private)
B. P. 584
Ouagadougou

ZAIRE[12]
Elima
(Government)
B. P. 10017
Kinshasa
Mambenga
(Government)
B. P. 197
Mbandake
Mwanga
(Government)
B. P. 2474
Lubumbashi
Salongo
(Government)
B. P. 601
Limete

ZAMBIA
Daily Mail
(Government)
P. O. Box 1421
Lusaka
Times of Zambia[13]
(Private)
P. O. Box 69
Mdola

NOTES

1. La Presse du Cameroun will suspend publication when the government begins two new daily newspapers in association with private interests. The French-language daily is titled La Tribune Camerounaise; the Cameroon Tribune will be the English-language daily.

2. The Congo once had three privately owned dailies, but they have disappeared as the nation has organized along Marxist lines.

3. The Evening News began publication on October 8, 1973 and is printed on the presses of the East African Standard. The proprietor is Narian Singh, who is also associated with the Sunday Post, a Kenya newspaper of long standing.

4. Daily Times is privately owned, but President H. Kamuzu Banda owns the majority of shares.

5. It is difficult to get an accurate count of the daily newspapers in Nigeria at any one time. The Texas-sized country has many population centers where daily newspapers spring up and later cease publication. The newspapers on this list represent the best information available as of March 1974.

6. The Morning Post folded in 1973 but reports indicate that the newspaper is now being published again.

7. Nigerian Chronicle became a daily in 1974.

8. Nigerian Standard became a daily in 1974.

9. The list of daily newspapers for Tanzania does not include those published on the island of Zanzibar.

10. Munno suspended publication in 1972 but reports indicate that it is now being published again.

11. The Voice of Uganda is the name now given to the former Uganda Argus, which was nationalized.

12. The names of Zaïre's daily newspapers reflect Africanization in 1973; the newspapers previously had French-based names.

13. The Times of Zambia is listed as a privately owned newspaper, but the government appoints the editor. Some reports indicate that the government now owns 51 percent of the newspaper, but this could not be confirmed.

Books

Agyemang, Eddie. "Freedom of Expression in a Government Newspaper in Ghana." In Reporting Africa, ed. Olav Stokke. Uppsala: Scandinavian Institute of African Affairs, 1971.

Ainslie, Rosalynde. The Press in Africa: Communications Past and Present. New York: Walker, 1966.

Apter, David E. Ghana in Transition. Princeton, N. J.: Princeton University Press, 1972.

Banks, Arthus S., and Robert B. Textor. A Cross Polity Survey. Cambridge, Mass.: MIT Press, 1963.

Barton, Frank. The Press in Africa. Nairobi: East Africa Publishing House, 1966.

Bates, Margaret L. "Tanganyika." In African One-Party States, ed. Gwendolen Carter. Ithaca, N. Y.: Cornell University Press, 1963.

Black, C. E. The Dynamics of Modernization. New York: Harper Torchbooks, 1966.

Browne, Don R. "Africa Overview." In National and International Systems of Broadcasting: Their History, Operation and Control, ed. Walter Emery. East Lansing: Michigan State University Press, 1969.

Clapham, Christopher S. Haile-Selassie's Government. New York: Praeger Publishers, 1970.

Coleman, James S. "Nationalism in Tropical Africa." In Independent Black Africa: The Politics of Freedom, ed. William J. Hanna. Chicago: Rand McNally, 1964.

_____ "The Politics of Sub-Saharan Africa." In The Politics of the Developing Areas, eds. Gabriel A. Almond and James S. Coleman. Princeton, N. J.: Princeton University Press, 1960.

Cowan, L. Gray. "Guinea." In African One-Party States, ed. Gwen-
    dolen Carter. Ithaca, N.Y.: Cornell University Press, 1963.

Daura, Mamman. "Editing a Government Newspaper in Nigeria." In
    Reporting Africa, ed. Olav Stokke. Uppsala: Scandinavian Insti-
    tute of African Affairs, 1971.

Deutsch, Karl W., and William J. Foltz, eds. Nation Building. New
    York: Aldine-Atherton, 1963.

Deutsch, Karl W. Nationalism and Social Communication. Cambridge,
    Mass.: MIT Press, 1966.

Dizard, Wilson. Television: A World View. Syracuse, N.Y.: Syracuse
    University Press, 1966.

Dodson, Don. "When Government Controls (Abroad)." In The Adversaries
    ed. William R. Rivers. Boston: Beacon Press, 1970.

Elias, T. O., ed. Nigerian Press Law. London: Evans Brothers, 1969.

Emerson, Rupert. "Nation Building in Africa." In Nation Building, eds.
    Karl W. Deutsch and William J. Foltz. New York: Aldine-Atherton,
    1963.

First, Ruth. "Political and Social Problems of Development." In Africa
    South of the Sahara. London: Europa Publications, 1972.

Fisher, Harold. "Interviewing Cross-Culturally." In Intercommunication
    Among Nations and Peoples, ed. Michael Prosser. New York:
    Harper and Row, 1973.

Githii, George. "Press Freedom in Kenya." In Reporting Africa, ed.
    Olav Stokke. Uppsala: Scandinavian Institute of African Affairs,
    1971.

Green, Timothy. The Universal Eye. New York: Stein and Day, 1972.

Hachten, William A. Muffled Drums. Ames: Iowa State University
    Press, 1971.

Kahl, Joseph. "Some Social Concomitants of Industrialization and
    Urbanization." In Independent Black Africa: The Politics of Free-
    dom, ed. William J. Hanna. Chicago: Rand McNally, 1964.

Kahn, Ely J. The First Decade: A Report on Independent Black Africa.
    New York: W. W. Norton, 1972.

Khaketla, B. M. Lesotho 1970–An African Coup Under the Microscope.
    Berkeley: University of California Press, 1972.

Kilson, Martin L. "Forces in Modern West Africa." In Twentieth Cen-
    tury Africa, ed. P. J. M. McEwan. London: Oxford University
    Press, 1968.

Kitchen, Helen, ed. The Press in Africa. Washington, D. C.: Ruth
    Sloan Associates, 1956.

LaVine, Victor T. The Cameroon Federal Republic. Ithaca, N.Y.:
    Cornell University Press, 1971.

Legum, Colin. "The Mass Media–Institutions of the African Political
    Systems." In Reporting Africa, ed. Olav Stokke. Uppsala: The
    Scandinavian Institute of African Affairs, 1971.

Lusignan, Guy de. French Speaking Africa Since Independence. London:
    Pall Mall, 1969.

Malinowski, B. "Dynamics of Social Change." In Social Change: The
    Colonial Situation, ed. Immanuel Wallerstein. New York: John
    Wiley and Sons, 1966.

Mazrui, Ali A. Cultural Engineering and Nation-Building in East Africa.
    Evanston, Ill.: Northwestern University Press, 1972.

Merrill, John C.; Carter R. Bryan; and Marvin Alisky. The Foreign
    Press. Baton Rouge: Louisiana State University Press, 1970.

Merrill, John C., and Ralph L. Lowenstein. Media Messages and Men–
    New Perspectives in Communication. New York: David McKay, 1971.

Morrison, Donald George; Robert Cameron Mitchell; John Naber Paden;
    and Hugh Michael Stevenson. Black Africa: A Comparative Hand-
    book. New York: The Free Press, 1972.

Nixon, Raymond. "Factors Related to Freedom in National Press Sys-
    tems." In International Communication, eds. Heinz-Dietrich
    Fischer and John C. Merrill. New York: Hastings House, 1970.

Ostheimer, John M. Nigerian Politics. New York: Harper and Row, 1973.

Patel, D. B. "Mass Communication and the Development of Africa."
    In Africa in World Affairs, eds. Ali A. Mazrui and Hasu H. Patel.
    New York: The Third Press, 1973.

Pye, Lucian W. Communications and Political Development. Princeton, N.J.: Princeton University Press, 1963.

Rice, Berkeley. Enter Gambia: The Birth of an Improbable Nation. Boston: Houghton Mifflin, 1967.

Rivkin, Arnold. Nation Building in Africa. New Brunswick, N.J.: Rutgers University Press, 1969.

Schramm, Wilbur. "Communication Development and the Development Process." In Communications and Political Development, ed. Lucian W. Pye. Princeton, N.J.: Princeton University Press, 1963.

Shils, Edward. "Intellectuals, Public Opinion, and Economic Development." In Independent Black Africa: The Politics of Freedom, ed. William J. Hanna. Chicago: Rand McNally, 1964.

Soja, Edward W. "Communications and Change." In The African Experience—Essays, vol. 1, eds. John N. Paden and Edward W. Soja. Evanston, Ill.: Northwestern University Press, 1970.

Drake, Clair St. "Traditional Authority and Social Action in Former British West Africa." In Independent Black Africa: The Politics of Freedom, ed. William J. Hanna. Chicago: Rand McNally, 1964.

Stokke, Olav. "Mass Communication in Africa—Freedoms and Functions." In Reporting Africa, ed. Olav Stokke. Uppsala: Scandinavian Institute of African Affairs, 1971.

_____. "The Mass Media in Africa and Africa in the International Mass Media—An Introduction." In Reporting Africa, ed. Olav Stokke. Uppsala: Scandinavian Institute of African Affairs, 1971.

Taylor, Charles Lewis, and Michael C. Hudson, eds. World Handbook of Political and Social Indicators. New Haven: Yale University Press, 1972.

Thompson, Virginia. The Emerging States of French Equatorial Africa. Stanford, Calif.: Stanford University Press, 1960.

Thompson, Virginia, and Richard Adloff, Djibouti and the Horn of Africa. Stanford, Calif.: Stanford University Press, 1968.

U.S. Army Area Handbook for Burundi. Washington, D.C.: Foreign Area Studies Division, American University, 1969.

U.S. Army Area Handbook for Chad. Washington, D.C.: Foreign Area Studies Division, American University, 1973.

U. S. Army Area Handbook for the People's Republic of the Congo (Brazzaville). Washington, D. C.: Foreign Area Studies Division, American University, 1971.

U. S. Army Handbook for the Democratic Republic of the Congo (Congo Kinshasa). Washington, D. C.: Foreign Area Studies Division, American University, 1971.

U. S. Army Area Handbook for Ethiopia. Washington, D. C.: Foreign Area Studies Division, American University, 1971.

U. S. Army Area Handbook for Ghana. Washington, D. C.: Foreign Area Studies Division, American University, 1971.

U. S. Army Area Handbook for Kenya. Washington, D. C.: Foreign Area Studies Division, American University, 1967.

U. S. Army Area Handbook for Liberia. Washington, D. C.: Foreign Area Studies Division, American University, 1972.

U. S. Army Area Handbook for Mauritania. Washington, D. C.: Foreign Area Studies Division, American University, 1972.

U. S. Army Area Handbook for Nigeria. Washington, D. C.: Foreign Area Studies Division, American University, 1972.

U. S. Army Area Handbook for Rwanda. Washington, D. C.: Foreign Area Studies Division, American University, 1969.

U. S. Army Area Handbook for Senegal. Washington, D. C.: Foreign Area Studies Division, American University, 1963.

U. S. Army Area Handbook for Somalia. Washington, D. C.: Foreign Area Studies Division, American University, 1970.

U. S. Army Area Handbook for the Democratic Republic of the Sudan. Washington, D. C.: Foreign Area Studies Division, American University, 1973.

U. S. Army Area Handbook for Tanzania. Washington, D. C.: Foreign Area Studies Division, American University, 1968.

U. S. Army Area Handbook for Zambia. Washington, D. C.: Foreign Area Studies Division, American University, 1969.

Van Bol, Jean-Marie, and Abdelfattah Fakhfakh. The Use of Mass Media in the Developing Countries—A Bibliography. Brussels: International Centre for African Social and Economic Documentation, 1971.

Weiner, Myron. "Political Integration and Political Development." In Political Development and Social Change, eds. Jason Finkle and Richard Gable. New York: John Wiley & Sons, 1971.

Williams, Francis. The Right to Know: The Rise of the World's Press. London: Longmans, 1969.

Woronoff, Jon. West African Wager: Houphouet versus Nkrumah. Metuchen, N.J.: Scarecrow Press, 1972.

Zolberg, Aristide R. Creating Political Order: The Party-States of West Africa. Chicago: Rand McNally, 1966.

Yearbooks

Africa South of the Sahara. London: Europa, 1972.

Broadcasting Yearbook. Wasington, D.C.: Broadcasting Publications, 1973.

Editor & Publisher International Yearbook. New York: Editor & Publisher, 1973.

Feuereisen, Fritz, and Ernst Schmache, eds. The Press in Africa. Munich: Verlag Dokumentation, 1973.

Legum, Colin ed. Africa Contemporary Record—Annual Survey and Documents. New York: Africana, 1973.

Newspaper Press Directory and Advertiser's Guide. London: Benn Brothers, 1973.

Nigeria Handbook. Lagos: Federal Ministry of Information, 1973.

The Official Associated Press Almanac. New York: Almanac, 1973.

UNESCO Statistical Yearbook 1971. Paris: UNESCO, 1972.

Articles

"Accused Risk a Year in Prison. " IPI Report, February 1969, p. 5.

"A Decade After Independence, Two Africans Meet. " IPI Report, April
    1971, pp. 1-3.

"A Genuinely Black State. " Time, December 18, 1972, p. 40 (Uganda).

Alabi, Aremu. "Tap of High Authority. " IPI Report, February 1973, p. 1.

Alexandre, Pierre. "Understanded of Which People—The Politics of
    Language. " Africa Report, July-August 1973, pp. 16-20.

Andoh, Isacc Fritz. "Democracy Returns to Ghana—Does It Mean Press
    Freedom?" IPI Report, December 1969, p. 8.

Ching, James C. "Mass Communications in the Republic of the Congo
    (Leopoldville). " Journalism Quarterly 41 (Spring 1964): 237-44.

Ciroma, Adamu. "The Risk That the Good Must Take. " IPI Report,
    July-August 1971, pp. 18-20.

Coker, Increase H. E. "Government Sponsors the Competition. "
    IPI Report, June 1968, pp. 16-17.

Coltart, James M. "The Influence of Newspapers and Television in
    Africa. " African Affairs 62 (July 1964): 202-10.

Condon, John. "Nation Building and Image Building in the Tanzania
    Press. " The Journal of Modern African Studies 5, no. 3 (1967):
    335-54.

Condon, John C. "Some Guidelines for Mass Communications Research
    in East Africa. " Gazette 14, no. 2 (1968): 141-51

Cotter, William R. "Africa: Not a Happy Year. " Freedom at Issue
    (Freedom House), January-February 1973, pp. 16-18.

Cowan, L. Gray. "Report of the Committee on Change in Intellectual
    Perspectives. " Issue: A Quarterly Journal of Africanist Opinion 2
    (Winter 1972): 1-5.

Crawford, Doug. "Africa's Airwaves: The Medium and the Message. "
    African Development, November 1979, pp. 18-19.

Davies, Derek, et al. "The State of the Press." Far Eastern Economic Review, October 9, 1971, pp. 21-24, 27, 50, 53.

Doob, Leonard W. "Information Service in Central Africa," Public Opinion Quarterly 17 (Spring 1953): 6-19.

"Dr. Banda Versus the Press." IPI Report, September-October 1973, pp. 1-2.

Dumoga, John W. K. "Getting the News is Only Half the Battle." IPI Report, June 1968, pp. 13-14.

Eapen, K.E. "Zana, An African News Agency." Gazette 18, no. 2 (1972): 193-207.

Edeani, David O. "Ownership and Control of the Press in Africa." Gazette 16, no. 2 (1970): 56-66.

Gallay, Pierre. "The English Missionary Press of East and Central Africa," Gazette 14, no. 2 (1968): 129-39.

Gbadoe, Mathias. "Immediate Freedom of the Press in Emergent Nations: Yes or No?" The Journalist's World 3, no. 1 (1965): 4-6.

Glaser, William A. "International Mail Surveys of Informants." Human Organization 25 (Spring 1966): 78-86.

Hachten, William A. "The Training of African Journalists." Gazette 14, no. 2 (1968): 101-10.

Hachten, William A. "Newspapers in Africa: Change or Decay," Africa Report, December 1970, pp. 25-28.

_____ "The Press in a One-Party State: The Ivory Coast Under Houphouet," Journalism Quarterly 44 (Spring 1967): 107-113.

_____ "The Press in a One-Party State: Kenya Since Independence." Journalism Quarterly 42 (Spring 1965): 262-66.

Hall, Richard. "The Press in Black Africa: How Free Is It?" Optima 18 (March 1968): 13-19.

_____ "Why the Independent Papers Are Few." IPI Report, June 1968, pp. 11-12.

Hitchcock, Robert. "Objectivity May Get Short Measure." IPI Report, December 1971, p. 1.

Holborn, Louise, W. "The Repatriation and Resettlement of the Southern Sudanese." Issue: A Quarterly Journal of Africanist Opinion 2 (Winter 1972): 23-26.

Hopkinson, Tom. "A New Age of Newspapers in Africa." Gazette 14, no. 2 (1968): 79-84.

Howe, Russell Warren. "Reporting from Africa: A Correspondent's View." Journalism Quarterly 43 (Summer 1966): 314-18.

Jaja, Emmanual A. "Problems of an African Editor." Africa Report, January 1966, pp. 40-42.

Jensen, Jay. "A Method and a Perspective for Criticism of the Mass Media." Journalism Quarterly 37 (Spring 1960): 261-66.

"Kaunda in Command." Time, October 8, 1973, p. 53.

Kent, Kurt E. "Freedom of the Press: An Empirical Analysis of One Aspect of the Concept." Gazette 18, no. 2 (1972): 65-75.

"Kenya Papers Warned of Split Loyalty." IPI Report, February 1969, p. 2.

Kenyatta, M. J. "An Address to the International Press Institute Conference in Nairobi," Africa Today 16, no. 3 (1969): 5-6.

Leech, John. "Zambia Seeks a Route to Fuller Independence." Issue: A Quarterly Journal of Africanist Opinion 2 (Winter 1972): 6-11.

"Lord High Everything." Time, March 4, 1974, p. 39 (Central African Republic).

Magloe, Theodore. "The African Press: Its Role." The Journalist's World 3, no. 4 (1965-66): pp. 22-25.

Makosso, Gabriel. "Congo's Voice." IPI Report, September 1968, p. 10.

Marsden, Eric. "The White Journalist in Black Africa." IPI Report, December 1970, pp. 8-9.

Merrill, John C. "Just What Kind of Newspapers for Developing Countries?" Journalist's World 5, no. 2 (1967): 21-22.

Meyer, Ernest. "Press Freedom in 1970: Under Seige From All Quarters." IPI Report, January 1973, pp. 1-8.

Mlenga, Kelvin G. "What Sort of Press Freedom?" The Journalist's World 3, no. 2 (1965): 14-17.

Mowlana, Hamid "Toward a Theory of Communication Systems," Gazette 17, nos. 1, 2, pp. 17-28.

Makupo, Titus. "What Role for the Government in the Development of an African Press?" Africa Report, January 1966, pp. 39-40.

Mytton, Graham L. "Tanzania: The Problems of Media Development." Gazette 14, no. 2 (1968): 89-100.

Ng'weno, Hilary B. "The Nature of the Threat to Press Freedom in East Africa." Africa Today 16, no. 3 (1969): 13-28.

Nixon, Raymond B. "Factors Related to Freedom in National Press Systems." Journalism Quarterly 37 (Winter 1960): 13-28.

_____ "Freedom in the World's Press: A Fresh Appraisal with New Data." Journalism Quarterly 42 (Winter 1965): 3-14, 118-19.

Omu, Fred I. A. "The Dilemma of Press Freedom in Colonial Africa: The West African Example." Journal of African History 9, no. 2 (1968): 279-98.

Oton, Esaukema Udo. "The Press of Liberia." Journalism Quarterly 38. (Spring 1961): 209-12.

Patel, Hasu H. "General Amin and the Indian Exodus." Issue: A Quarterly Journal of Africanist Opinion 2 (Winter 1972): 12-22.

Paterson, Adolphus A. "Ghana Council Raises Hopes—And Fears." IPI Report, February 1968, p. 7.

Paterson, Adolphus A. "Why Africa Needs a Free Press." Africa Report, April 1971, pp. 22-24.

"President Kenyatta Airs Ownership Question." IPI Report, July-August 1968, pp. 10-11.

"Role for Unity—If Press Has Freedom to Play It." IPI Report, July-August 1968, pp. 10-11.

Russell, Nick. "Tabloid and Broadsheet Face Same Odds." IPI Report, June 1968, pp. 15-16.

Smith, Jasper K. "The Press and Elite Values in Ghana, 1962-70."
     Journalism Quarterly 49 (Winter 1972): 679-83.

Sommerlad, E. Lloyd. "Problems in Developing a Free Enterprise Press
     in East Africa." Gazette 14, no. 2 (1968): 74-78.

"Speedy at Work." Time, April 23, 1973, p. 31 (Liberia).

"Survival Struggle in Africa." IPI Report, February 197.3, pp. 1-3.

"The Comparative Survey of Freedom," Freedom at Issue (Freedom
     House), January-February 1973, p. 4.

"Togo's Free Press Lasts 15 Issues." IPI Report, February 1968, p. 3.

"Tradition Means the King." Africa Report, July-August 1973, pp. 26-27.
     (Swaziland).

"Uganda Editor Jailed, Cleared, Jailed Again." IPI Report, March 1969,
     p. 2.

Ugboajah, Francis Okwuadigbo. "Traditional-Urban Media Model:
     Stocktaking for African Development." Gazette 18, no. 2 (1972):
     76-95.

"Voices on the African Air." African Development, December 1969, p. 24.

Weinstein, Warren. "Tensions in Burundi." Issue: A Quarterly of
     Africanist Opinion 2 (Winter 1972): 27-29.

"What Did Amakari Do?" IPI Report, September-Octover 1973, pp. 1-2, 16.

"Where Images Matter, Bans Are Risk." IPI Report, July-August 1968,
     pp. 15-16.

Published Reports

Coker, O. S. "Mass Media in Nigeria." In Perspectives on Mass
     Media Systems, ed. Royal D. Colle. Report compiled by the
     Department of Communication Arts, New York State Colleges of
     Agriculture. Ithaca, N.Y.: Cornell University Press, 1968.

Communications Media and Africa. "The Development of Information
     and Techniques of Diffusion in Africa." Special report (No. 90-91)

prepared by Interstages. Brussels: Belgian Institute of Information
and Documentation, October 1973.

_____ Report of the Washington Task Force on Africa. Washington, D. C.
African Bibliographic Center, 1973.

Dodson, Don, and William Hachten. Communication and Development:
African and Afro-American Parallels. Journalism Monographs, no. 28
(May 1973). Lexington, Ky: Association for Education in Journalism.

Eapen, K. E. The Media and Development: An Exploratory Survey in
Indonesia and Zambia With Special Reference to the Role of the
Churches. Report prepared by the Centre for Mass Communication
Research at the University of Leicester, England, for the World
Association for Christian Communication. Leeds: J. A. Kavangh
and Sons, 1973.

Foreign Newspaper Report. No. 3. Washington, D. C.: Library of Congress, 1973.

Hachten, William. Mass Communications in Africa: An Annotated
Bibliography. Madison: Center for International Communication
Studies, University of Wisconsin, 1971.

Healey, Joseph G. Press Freedom in Kenya. Columbia: Freedom of
Information Center at the University of Missouri, 1967.

Mazrui, Ali A. "The Press, Intellectuals and the Printed Word." In
Mass Thoughts, eds. Edward Moyo and Susan Raynor. Kampala:
Makerere University, 1972.

Nelson, D. "Government and the Free Press." In Mass Thoughts,
eds. Edward Moyo and Susan Raynor. Kampala: Makerere University, 1972.

Ogunbi, Adebayo. A Select Bibliography on Communication in Africa.
East Lansing: Department of Radio and Television at Michigan
State University, 1973.

Ojera, A. A. "The Press in Africa: Is It Dying?" In Mass Thoughts,
eds. Edward Moyo and Susan Raynor. Kampala: Makerere University, 1972.

Republican Sierra Leone. Freetown: Government Information Services
(no date).

Resident Foreign Media: Press, TV, Radio Correspondents in the United
    States. Washington, D.C.: Foreign Press Center of United States
    Information Agency, July 1973.

Rose, E. J. B. Problems of the Press in Africa. Munster: Institute of
    Mass Communication at Munster University, 1962.

Selected Economic Data for the Less Developed Countries. Office of
    Statistics and Reports, Bureau for Program and Policy Coordination.
    Washington, D.C: Agency for International Development, 1972.

Traber, Michael. "Kiongozi of Tanzania: Development for Self-Reliance."
    Mimeo press survey of restricted circulation compiled for the
    Department of Communications, Tanzania Episcopal Conference
    in cooperation with the Catholic Media Council and the Lenten
    Fund of the Bishop's Conference of the Netherlands. Kitwe, Zambia:
    Africa Literature Center, 1973.

Newspaper Articles

"A Nonconformist Finds Africa Hard." New York Times, April 23, 1972.

"Censoring Stories: African Style." Washington Post, March 28, 1972.

"The Crunch on African Newspapers." San Francisco Chronicle, August
    15, 1973.

"Dahomey Reports Ex-Chief Jailed." New York Times, October 29, 1972.

"Freedom of Expression Taking Hold in Liberia." New York Times,
    October 28, 1973.

"Guineans Backing President's Plan." New York Times, February 25, 1972.

"Nigeria's Press Large and Active." New York Times, February 24, 1974.

"Swaziland Vote Lessens Royalist Rule." New York Times, May 21, 1972.

"Upper Volta Leader Explains Take-Over." New York Times, February
    10, 1974.

"Zambia Worries About Fifth Column." Washington Post, March 11, 1972.

Unpublished Material

Bunge, Walter. "Some Aspects of Press Law in Africa." Paper presented
     to the Association for Education in Journalism annual meeting,
     Berkeley, Calif., August 1969.

Cutter, Charles. "Political Communication in a Pre-Literate Society:
     The Radio in Mali." Paper presented to the African Studies Asso-
     ciation annual meeting, Denver, Colo., November 3, 1971.

Findlay, Joseph W. O. "A Comparative Study of Broadcasting Research
     in Some Commonwealth African Countries During the Period 1960-65."
     Master's thesis, University of Iowa, 1971.

Hanson, John H. "The Press in Liberia." Master's thesis, Syracuse
     University, 1972.

Healey, Joseph. "Mass Media Growth in Kenya." Master's thesis,
     University of Missouri, 1968.

Hobbs, Daryl J. "Patterns of Communication in Malawi." Paper pre-
     pared for University of Missouri AID project in Malawi; Columbia,
     1966.

Jose, Alhaji Babatunde. "The Press in Nigeria." Paper presented to the
     opening session of Distripress in Athens, Greece, October 23, 1973.

Kucera, Geoffrey Z. "Broadcasting in Africa: A Study of Belgian, Bri-
     tish, and French Colonial Policies." Ph. D. dissertation, Michigan
     State University, 1968.

Lowenstein, Ralph L. "Measuring World Press Freedom as a Political
     Indicator." Ph. D. dissertation, University of Missouri, 1967.

Masha, F. L. "Attitudes of African Students Towards the Relationship
     Between the Government and the Press in Africa: A Factor Analytic
     Study." Master's thesis, Southern Illinois University, 1970.

Nwankwo, Robert L. "Utopia and Reality in the African Mass Media:
     A Case Study." Paper presented at the African Studies Association
     annual meeting, Philadelphia, Pa., November 9, 1972.

Miller, Norman N. "Kenya: Nationalism and the Press 1951-61."
     Master's thesis, Indiana University, 1962.

Ronen, Dov. "Political Development in a West African Country: The Case of Dahomey." Ph. D. dissertation, Indiana University, 1969.

Roppa, Guy M. "Communication for Modernization in a Nomadic Society: Conditions and Prospects in Somalia." Master's thesis, Indiana University, 1970.

Seawell, John Patrick. "Mass Communication in Ethiopia: Blunted Instrument of Government." Master's theeis, University of Texas, 1971.

Wilhelm, John. "List of Foreign Correspondent Abroad Employed by American Media." Copy supplied by College of Communication at Ohio University, Athens, 1973.

Letters

Alpern, Stanley B., of United State Information Service, Ouagadougou, Upper Volta (October 2, 1972).

Arnaud, Andre, of embassy of France, Washington, D. C. (October 30, 1973).

Bailey, Berton M., of U. S. Information Service, Maseru, Lesotho (November 5, 1973).

Baker-Bates, M. S., of British embassy in Washington, D. C. (November 14, 1973).

Bennett, George, of Africa Literature Centre, Kitwe, Zambia (September 21, 1973).

Bontrager, Robert D., of Department of Journalism at Kansas State University, Manhattan (October 15, 1973).

Brinkman, Del, of William Allen White School of Journalism, University of Kansas, Lawrence (October 18, 1973).

Clarke, Walter S., of U. S. Department of State, Douala, Cameroon (January 29, 1974).

Cochet, M.,of embassy of France, Lome, Togo, (January 3, 1974).

Day, J. Laurence, of William Allen White School of Journalism, University of Kansas, Lawrence (November 5, 1973).

Dizard, Wilson P., of U.S. Information Agency, Washington, D.C. (September 28, 1973).

Donnelley, M. Simon, of Multimedia Zambia, Lusaka, Zambia (January 15, 1974).

Fullerton, A. G., of UNESCO Regional Office for Education in Africa, Dakar, Senegal (October 9, 1973 and October 22, 1973).

Galipeau, George, of Center for the Study of Science and Techniques of Information, University of Dakar, Senegal (Novermber 5, 1973).

Hachten, William A., of School of Journalism at the University of Wisconsin, Madison (November 3, 1973).

Hart, Norman, of Africa Acts feature service, Nairobi, Kenya (September 19, 1973).

Head, Sydney W., of School of Communications at Temple University, Philadelphia (November 7, 1973).

Hopkinson, Tom, of Department of Journalistic Studies at the University College, Cardiff, Wales (October 17, 1973 and December 13, 1973).

Hovanec, Vincent J., of U.S. Information Service, Libreville, Gabon (November 2, 1973).

Hunter, Frederic, of Christian Science Monitor, Boston (January 5, 1974).

Jaffe, Andrew, of Newsweek, Nairobi, Kenya (January 28, 1974).

Kazinja, L. M. S., of School of Journalism in the Uganda Ministry of Information, Kampala (November 10, 1973).

Kotok, Alan, of U.S. Information Agency, Washington, D.C. (July 30, 1973).

Kugblenu, John S., of Radio Review and TV Times, Accra, Ghana (December 10, 1973).

Legum, Colin, of The Observer, London (September 21, 1972).

Loubendje, J., of l'Agence Gabonaise de Presse, Libreville, Gabon (January 28, 1974).

McCarthy, Michael, of Trinity and All Saints Colleges, Leeds, United
    Kingdon (January 8, 1974).

McAteer, William H., of School of Journalism at the University of
    Nairobi, Kenya (October 22, 1973).

McHale, James D., of U. S. Information Service, Niamey, Niger (Nov-
    ember 5, 1973).

Mack, James L., of U. S. Information Service, Mogadiscio, Somali
    Democratic Republic (December 8, 1973).

Martin, John L., of College of Journalism at the University of Maryland,
    College Park (July 24, 1973).

Massieu, C., of Office de Radiodiffusion-Television Francaise (ORTF),
    Paris (February 25, 1974).

Motuba, Edgar M., of Leselinyana La Lesotho, Morija, Lesotho (Dec-
    ember 20, 1973).

Mowlana, Hamid, of School of International Service at the American
    University, Washington, D. C. (September 11, 1973).

Navaux, Pierre, of UNESCO Office for Research and Planning of Com-
    munication, Paris (August 6, 1973).

Odukomaiya, Henyr O., of Daily Times Group, Lagos, Nigeria (February
    18, 1974).

Peel, Richard, of International Press Institute, Zurich, Switzerland
    (October 17, 1973).

Philip, Anne, of Centre International d'Enseignement Superieur du
    Journalisme, Strasbourg, France (September 28, 1973).

Pierce-Goulding, T., of Commonwealth Press Union, London (September
    12, 1973).

Razi, G. Michael, of U. S. Information Service, N-Djamena (Fort Lamy),
    Chad (October 31, 1973).

Robertson, E. H., of World Association for Christian Communication,
    London (August 15, 1973).

Ross, Sherman H., of U. S. Information Service, Cotonou, Dahomey
    (November 9, 1973).

Rotundo, Vincent, of U. S. Information Service, Lome, Togo (November 12, 1973).

Rowlands, D. G. H., of Thomson Foundation Editorial Study Centre, Cardiff, Wales (October 1, 1973 and January 24, 1974).

Ryan, Henry A., of U. S. Information Service, Conakry, Guinea (November 1, 1973).

Sargent, Leslie W., of United Nations Development Programme, Georgetown, Guyana (October 30, 1973).

Scotten, James F., of Institute of Mass Communication at the University of Lagos, Nigeria (July 11, 1973).

Scotten, James F., of York College of the City University of New York, Jamaica, N. Y. (October 30, 1973).

Shumaker, C. Richard, of Evangelical Literature Office, Sugar Grove, Ill. (September 19, 1973).

Wilhelm, John R., of College of Communication at Ohio University, Athens, (August 16, 1973).

Interviews

Adjoyi, William Koffi, counselor at embassy of Togo, Washington, D. C. (January 9, 1974).

Almeida, Innocent Paulin, press attache at embassy of Dahomey, Washington, D. C. (January 2, 1974).

Aziz, Hamza, counselor of political affairs at embassy of Tanzania, Washington, D. C. (January 7, 1974).

Brobey, K. A., counselor of information at embassy of Ghana, Washington, D. C. (January 3, 1974).

Changawa, Arthur, third secretary of embassy of Kenya, Washington, D. C. (January 7, 1974).

Coulibaly, Sayon, counselor at embassy of Mali, Washington, D. C. (January 7, 1974).

Dambatta, Magaji, counselor at embassy of Nigeria, Washington, D. C. (January 7, 1974).

Dhlamini, David M. H., first secretary at embassy of Swaziland, Washington, D. C. (January 2, 1974).

El Tayeb, Hassan A., cultural counselor at embassy of Sudan, Washington, D. C. (January 2, 1974).

Fagla, Hubert, visiting journalist from Dahomey, Columbia, Missouri (September 13, 1973).

Kla-Williams, Temynors, press counselor at embassy of Liberia, Washington, D. C. (January 4, 1974).

Kourouma, Fouroumo, counselor at embassy of Guinea, Washington, D. C. (January 4, 1974).

Mapangou, Simon, first secratary at embassy of Gabon, Washington, D. C. (January 8, 1974).

Mbale, Rodwell M. K., minister at embassy of Malawi, Washington, D. C. (January 3, 1974).

Mekbib, Ghebeyehou, first secretary at embassy of Ethiopia, Washington, D. C. (January 10, 1974).

Molapo, Konka Consalo, first secretary at embassy of Lesotho, Washington, D. C. (January 8, 1974).

Mpuchane, Samuel A., first secretary at embassy of Botswana, Washington, D. C. (January 4, 1974).

Munyeshyaka, Ildenphonse, first secretary at embassy of Rwanda, Washington, D. C. (January 11, 1974).

Mwanza, Ferdinand E., first secretary at embassy of Zambia, Washington, D. C. (January 9, 1974).

N'Gensi, N'Gambani Zi Mizele, first secretary at embassy of Zaïre, Washington, D. C. (January 7, 1974).

Njosa, Simon, press attache at embassy of Cameroon, Washington, D. C. (January 3, 1974).

Oluka, Alex Mackey, third secretary at embassy of Uganda, Washington, D. C. (January 7, 1974).

Ould Lidi, Mekhalle, second secretary at embassy of Mauritania, Washington, D. C. (January 8, 1974).

Sisso, Dominique B., counselor at embassy of Upper Volta, Washington, D. C. (January 11, 1974).

Soloku, Julius V. L., information attaché at embassy of Sierra Leone, Washington, D. C. (January 9, 1974).

Visson, Anatole, press counselor at embassy of Ivory Coast, Washington, D. C. (January 3, 1974).

DENNIS L. WILCOX, a professor on the faculty of journalism at San Jose State University in California, has conducted mass media research in Western Europe, the Soviet Union, the South Pacific and Africa. He has written journal articles on the role of mass media in developing nations and is author of the book, English Language Dailies Abroad (1967).

Prior to his present position, Dr. Wilcox was on the faculty of the International Studies Division for Chapman College in California. He formerly was a reporter on newspapers in Colorado, a correspondent covering the Ohio Legislature and a public relations specialist for colleges and universities.

Dr. Wilcox received his B. A. in political science from the University of Denver and an M. A. in journalism from the University of Iowa. His Ph. D. in international communications is from the University of Missouri School of Journalism. Professional memberships include the African Studies Association and the International Press Institute in Zurich.

BROADCASTING TO THE SOVIET UNION: International
Politics and Radio
            Maury Lisann

CITIZENS' GROUPS AND BROADCASTING
            Donald Guimary

COMMUNICATIONS AND PUBLIC OPINION: A Public
Opinion Quarterly Reader
            Robert Carlson

MASS COMMUNICATION AND CONFLICT RESOLUTION:
The Role of the Information Media in the Advancement
of International Understanding
            W. Phillips Davison

PUBLIC ACCESS CABLE TELEVISION IN THE UNITED
STATES AND CANADA: With an Annotated Bibliography
            Gilbert Gillespie

THE USES OF COMMUNICATION IN DECISION-MAKING:
A Comparative Study of Yugoslavia and the United States
            Alex S. Edelstein